POLICY STUDIES IN EMPLOYMENT AND WELFARE NUMBER 9

General Editors: Sar A. Levitan and Garth L. Mangum

Social Experimentation and Manpower Policy: The Rhetoric and the Reality

Sar A. Levitan
Robert Taggart III

The Johns Hopkins Press, Baltimore and London

331.1
L666S

Copyright © 1971 by The Johns Hopkins Press
All rights reserved
Manufactured in the United States of America

The Johns Hopkins Press, Baltimore, Maryland 21218
The Johns Hopkins Press Ltd., London

Library of Congress Catalog Card Number 78-153557

International Standard Book Number 0-8018-1276-3 (clothbound edition)
International Standard Book Number 0-8018-1323-9 (paperback edition)

Originally published, 1971
Paperback edition, 1971

This study was prepared under a grant from The Ford Foundation.

Contents

Preface

As "credentialed experts" in the employ of a university center, we are occasionally asked the very simple questions: Do manpower programs work? Which are the most effective? In what directions should we be moving? These questions are basic, and answers are crucial in determining the size of manpower outlays and their allocation among programs.

Embarrassingly, our replies are usually ambiguous, guarded by the assertion that "it depends." Few stay to listen and to learn what it depends upon. Seeking the comfort of straightforward replies, they turn instead to those who supply answers rather than raise more questions.

This is not the way things were supposed to be. Manpower efforts were expanded in the belief that program performance could be measured and evaluated, alternative approaches compared, and rational decisions made in improving the programs and determining priorities. With refined techniques and accurate data, it was assumed that evaluators could provide relatively clearcut prescriptions. Rather than acting as occasional kibitzers, social scientists hoped that they would play a major role in policy formulation.

In retrospect, it seems clear that their expectations were inflated. In real life, program performance could not be accurately measured, evaluators disagreed in their appraisals, and the prescriptions for improvement were often complex and contradictory. To implement the programs, decisions had to be made before lessons could be learned; and though social scientists were given a hearing, they could provide few answers at the outset. As evidence accumulated and a case could be made for changes, their counsel was sometimes heeded but just as often ignored. With most research funds in the hands of program administrators, evaluators were often dissuaded from broad and critical investigations.

Social scientists accepted their narrow assignments, attacking with zest the specific tasks where their analytical tools could be applied with some precision. Many academic researchers were comfortable in this circumscribed environment since they could display virtuosity dabbling in the esoteric mysteries of numerology. Armed with cost-benefit techniques and shielded by the mantle of objectivity, they set out in search of holy grails. Like the knights of an earlier day, they failed to achieve the purity they sought; they returned more worldly wise, but without the object of their search.

Those who are familiar with manpower programs know that accurate measurement, objective evaluation, and carefully analyzed decisions have seldom been realized. Yet much that is written and spoken about manpower policy continues to ascribe an important role to these ingredients. Manpower authorities have been reluctant to share operational data with outsiders, who might then see the emperor's clothes for what they are. Several investigators have detailed the histories and performances of the different programs, indicating in each case the dearth of available data, the shortcomings of existing studies, and the ill-designed steps which have been taken. But few have drawn together and weighed these criticisms to get a realistic idea of the past and present contributions of measurement, evaluation, and carefully engineered change. Expectations of what these would accomplish and claims which are often made inflate the very real contributions of such methods.

The purpose of reviewing past, present, and likely future developments is not to reveal the emperor in his nakedness, but rather to find ways of increasing the contribution of social scientists to the manpower programs, highlighting the lessons we have learned so that mistakes will not be repeated, and critically examining claims which have been unquestioned. The analysis is meant to be constructive in replacing rhetoric with realism. The world is complex, and there are no simple ways to improve the design and administration of social programs; but marginal improvements are possible if the directions of change are pointed out and if program planners settle for less than "grand designs." This is difficult where both the future horizons and the past landmarks are clouded by misconceptions. To disperse these false notions does not insure improvement, but better progress is likely under clear skies.

This study ties together a number of program evaluations, methodological discussions, and policy analyses well known by those who have labored in the vineyard. The fact that these exist, and can serve as a basis for introspection, is itself an indication of the many contributions which have been made. Though this study provides little new knowledge, hopefully it will suggest different and alternative ways of viewing and organizing the substantial knowledge which already exists. Its intent is to provide a modest guide to the perplexed though not necessarily uninitiated, counter-balancing the simplistic arguments which have been and are being used in support of programs and policies. To aid those who are unfamiliar with the programs, an appendix is supplied which identifies their basic provisions.

Because old ideas and facts are discussed at great length, much has been borrowed. It would be impossible to mention all those who have contributed to the knowledge about manpower programs, and no attempt is made to "document" or to attribute sources to the materials used in this study. But clearly a debt of gratitude is owed to Garth Mangum, whose writings have been seminal. He also helped by reading and commenting on this manuscript, along with Roger Davidson of the University of California, Rashi Fein of Harvard University, Charles Myers of MIT, and Robert Schrank, consultant to The Ford Foundation. A number of Labor Department officials provided useful suggestions while voicing strong disagreement with many of the conclusions. They do not care to be identified, but we express our gratitude for their help.

This study was prepared under a grant from The Ford Foundation to The George Washington University's Center for Manpower Policy Studies. In accordance with the Foundation's practice, complete responsibility for the preparation of the volume has been left to the authors.

SAR A. LEVITAN
ROBERT TAGGART III

CENTER FOR MANPOWER POLICY STUDIES
THE GEORGE WASHINGTON UNIVERSITY

Social Experimentation and Manpower Policy:
The Rhetoric and the Reality

Where is the wisdom we have lost in knowledge?
Where is the knowledge we have lost in information?

The Rock
T. S. Eliot

1

The Search for Measurement and Evaluation

The decade of the 1960s was one of growth and change in many areas of social policy. The dramatic proliferation of manpower programs was one significant manifestation of the growing social responsibilities assumed by the government. Before 1961, only limited governmental funds were allocated to improve the functioning of the labor market and to provide remedial services for disadvantaged workers. At the beginning of the decade, there was no such thing as a manpower policy, or even a distinguishable set of manpower programs to help those who experienced difficulties in competing for sustained gainful employment. During the next ten years, however, federal efforts grew significantly in scale and in scope. Employment services, vocational education, and rehabilitation for the disabled were expanded and reshaped. A wide range of new programs and approaches were initiated providing training for the technologically displaced; public employment for youths, the aged, and those on welfare; subsidies to private employers to hire, train, and retain disadvantaged workers; residential vocational education for teenagers; basic education for adults; and many other services. Expenditures on these manpower programs increased more than tenfold over the decade, reaching a level of nearly $3 billion in fiscal 1970.

An important feature of these rapidly expanding manpower efforts was the attempt to improve upon the traditional methods of determining and implementing public policy. Under the manpower programs, perhaps more than in any other area, emphasis was placed on measuring and evaluating performance, comparing alternative approaches, and making decisions based on hard evidence rather than exhortation. Because of the unknown terrain, mistakes were anticipated; but through the application of more rigorous and objective analysis, it was hoped that these mistakes could be spotted and in the future avoided.

To these ends, measurement and evaluation were made an integral part of the manpower programs. The funds allocated specifically for these purposes were increased over the decade. By fiscal 1969, $21 million was spent for special experimental and demonstration projects, $5 million for government funded research, and $4 million for internal evaluation. Additionally, $73 million went for program administration, including the gathering of operational data, $32 million for the collection and publication of labor market information, and $10 million for technical assistance. Altogether, $153 million, or 6.4 percent of the total fiscal 1969 manpower outlays (excluding vocational education), went for program administration, research, or support, though the proportion has declined somewhat in fiscal 1970 and 1971. And these are only a part of the resources going into the evaluation of program performance. As the manpower effort expanded, more and more private researchers and research institutions became interested, and a wide range of studies have been made. Publications of all sorts have sprouted, with the number of manpower evaluators expanding rapidly.

It is not just the scale of these analytical efforts which has been important, but also the fact that a concerted attempt has been made to feed the results back into the design and administration of the programs. Not only are manpower data more detailed and accurate, evaluations more widespread, and experimental projects broader-ranging in scope than similar efforts in other areas, but in addition this information is directed to vital policy matters and is given careful consideration by administrators and legislators. Though sometimes ignored, the prescriptions suggested by analysis have been given more weight in formulating manpower strategies than in determining policies elsewhere.

From this perspective, the manpower programs can be viewed as some of the most conscious and far-reaching efforts at social experimentation. All the ingredients of a social experiment are there. To meet a recognized problem, alternative approaches were designed and implemented on the basis of prevailing assumptions and beliefs. Their effectiveness was then measured, evaluated, and compared. These assessments were, in turn, used to improve the design and mix of programs and to give some test to their underlying assumptions.

In the process, the success of the different manpower programs has been appraised on numerous occasions. But the experimental methods themselves have not been extensively analyzed, nor has their impact been assessed. Because the manpower programs have utilized these methods to a greater degree and with more success than other social programs, it is worthwhile to examine carefully their experience. The application of experimental methods under the manpower effort has itself been a social experiment. Evaluating the results can help to determine the applicability and promise of these techniques in other areas, and it can improve their application to the manpower programs.

It is a safe guess that the manpower programs would have been considerably less effective if the insights provided by measurement and evaluation had been ignored. There are documented cases where changes have been brought about on the basis of careful analyses and these have led to measurable improvements. While there are many other cases in which the experimental methods made little contribution to decision-making, there is no reason to think they had a negative impact. It is almost axiomatic that program performance will be improved if decisions are based on more accurate information, and there can be no doubt that much information has been generated by the application of experimental methods.

In trying to get a more exact measure of their impact, however, one is immediately confronted by a plethora of misconceptions and false claims. Many of these are inherent in looking at the programs as social experiments. Though they have elements of experimentation, the programs are primarily, if not exclusively, operational efforts concerned with solving specific pressing problems; they are only secondarily concerned with testing the efficacy of alternative approaches. Because of the vast number of factors influencing performance, the experimental aspects of the programs can yield few clearcut or unequivocal answers. These limitations are sometimes ignored in the quest for scientific purity, giving the idea that the design and operation of social programs is a more rational and exact process than it really can be. The methods of program evaluation also have limitations. Relevant data are often inadequate, and the analytical techniques have many shortcomings. The preoccupation of many analysts with esoteric mathematical techniques has contributed to arid exercises which pass for "rigid" analysis, though they are useless for policy formulation. Even where improvements can be suggested on the basis of evaluation, there are obstacles limiting the use of this information. Where other factors affect decisions, these are usually hidden behind a smokescreen of seemingly rational explanations, giving the impression that the choice has been well-grounded in hard facts. At all turns, policies and priorities are justified by claims of demonstrated effectiveness. Thus, the rhetoric of the manpower programs tends to exaggerate the impact of social experimentation. More unfortunately, it often clouds the picture so that needed improvements are not being made in the programs or in their experimental methods.

The claims and misconceptions shrouding manpower policy are difficult to pin down. For one thing, they usually contain an element of truth along with a large measure of exaggeration. Their origins are ambiguous—the combination of academic and other researchers buttering their bread, administrators justifying their skills, politicians wooing votes, and, above all, vested groups defending their interests. Those who perpetrate the myths will rarely admit to believing or initiating them, so that the critical observer is often left attacking straw men. But whatever the substance of these myths, and whether or not they are believed by their perpetrators, they have a significant influence on legislative, administrative, and academic thinking. It is only by exploding false claims and clearing up misconceptions that the impact of social experimentation can be determined and improved.

The rhetoric of manpower policy has exaggerated the impact of social experimentation and the rationality of manpower programs. To show the rhetoric for the exaggeration that it is does not imply that the experimental methods have been ineffective or the manpower programs irrational. The opposite is the case. It is only when measured against inflated claims that social experimentation or the manpower programs themselves have been a failure. Next to the rhetoric of manpower policy, reality may seem rather dim, but this is no reason to underestimate its impact or to turn away from the opportunities for improvement.

2

Testing Alternative Approaches

THE RHETORIC: The manpower programs have provided adequate tests of their alternative approaches.

THE REALITY: Many factors affect program performance, and these limit the conclusions which can be drawn from success or failure.

The view that manpower programs are a social experiment is more an ideal concept of social scientists than a primary aim or a realized goal of these efforts. The claim that is central to this study—that the manpower programs were intended as a test of alternative approaches, or at least that they served this purpose—overstates the importance of social experimentation. The lessons learned from the experience of manpower programs are subject to numerous caveats, and even the most rigid review of program experience is not adequate to test the underlying hypotheses upon which the efforts are based. Though this is a useful analytical framework, it distorts reality as much as any theory. At the outset, therefore, the limitations of the manpower programs as social experiments must be spelled out to avoid additional misconceptions.

The optimum experimental design is one in which all exogenous factors are either accounted for or held constant, a procedure unattainable in social science. Six variables tend to be critical under the manpower programs: (1) the ability and availability of program administrators and project leadership at the community level; (2) the political climate and the degree of support from vested interest groups; (3) the quality of the clientele which is served; (4) the adequacy of supportive services which are offered; (5) the economic circumstances in which the program or project operates; and (6) the timing and preparation for the mounting of the efforts. All of these factors can vary widely among projects, between the areas where they are applied, and over time. Unless these variations are carefully considered, the information provided by measurement and evaluation can be misapplied; and even if these factors are given the fullest attention, a wide margin of uncertainty must prevail.

EXPANDING AND EXPORTING SUCCESSFUL APPROACHES

The development of the Concentrated Employment Program (CEP) into a major manpower effort, with $189 million in federal obligations during fiscal 1970, is a prime illustration of the problems involved in using projects and programs as social experiments. Some of the basic concepts underlying CEP—its reliance on local business support, its delivery of manpower services in areas of greatest deprivation according to individual need, and its effort to follow up placements in order to help them stay on their jobs— were borrowed from the Jobs Now project in Chicago, which served as a prototype for similar efforts in other cities under CEP.

Jobs Now had been operating for a year prior to the initiation of CEP. Precipitated by the outbreak of violence in Chicago during the summer of 1966, the project aimed at placing young gang members in jobs offering opportunities for advancement. The YMCA administered the project, and it had long experienced working with youth groups and employers in trying to find jobs for disadvantaged youths. Because leading businessmen were members of, or were contacted by, the YMCA board, because further riots threatened, and because tight labor market conditions prevailed in Chicago, businessmen participated actively. All of these factors were important ingredients in the performance of the program, and it is doubtful that many other areas could have duplicated them.

Jobs Now recruited the most disadvantaged youth over 16 years of age, and the only grounds for rejection were obvious mental retardation, narcotics addiction or alcoholism, more than four months' pregnancy, or a pending court case. While "status" gang members were not or could not be recruited, the enrollees were clearly a hard-to-employ group, with three-fourths 19 years of age or less, a third with police records, only 7 percent with high school diplomas, and 98 percent Negro.

These enrollees were given a two-week program of counseling in an attempt to acquaint them with the world of work. They were then placed in jobs and followed-up in their progress. These jobs were provided voluntarily by industry, which often waived educational requirements or dropped rules against hiring ex-convicts, and in some cases provided training and counseling at their own expense.

Between September 1966 and May 1967, more than a thousand youths were enrolled in the project. In August 1967, 28 percent were employed, and 8 percent were in school, training, or the armed services, so that the success rate was 36 percent. An additional 30 percent were still in the program. In light of the clientele which was served, this was considered by evaluators and knowledgeable program operators to be a moderately good performance.

It is significant that when the administrators of Jobs Now were offered the opportunity to expand, they chose to limit growth to 25 percent. Their reasons were that the staff was limited, so that follow-up and job coaching were suffering, and an expanded staff would mean less experienced personnel. Perhaps more important, there was no indication that many more employers would be willing to provide the high level of support essential for the project.

Despite the recognized limits to expansion, and the very serious doubts about the replicability of the Jobs Now model, the CEP program was initiated with a greater concentration of resources. By the end of fiscal 1967, projects were funded in 20 urban slum areas and two rural depressed areas, and these were scheduled to provide services to an estimated 34,000 enrollees.

Considering the large outlays, the program hardly lived up to expectations. For one thing, businessmen in most cities did not play an active role. Most of the prime sponsors were community action agencies composed of indigenous leaders and having few attachments to the business community. Because of the large scale of enrollments and rapid implementation without planning or local consultation, an adequate number of jobs could not be generated which would provide a high level of support with no remuneration. There was also a shortage of experienced personnel to manage and staff the programs. Leadership in the CAAs could usually communicate with the clientele, taking an interest in their needs, but they found it difficult to deal with employers. Where the public employment service was the prime sponsor, employer relations were better but community relations suffered. The program was expanded so quickly that there was insufficient time to develop working relationships among the concerned agencies. Linkages with the schools and with MDTA were inadequate and often nonexistent. Where the Jobs Now concept evolved from careful thought and planning taking place in a single community, the CEP concept was only rough-hewn before it was implemented in cities with widely varying conditions.

Despite these shortcomings, the Concentrated Employment Program was further extended. By late 1968, 76 CEPs were operating, 13 of them in rural areas. One reason for expansion was the enthusiastic support of the Secretary of Labor, who was committed to the CEP approach and favored the program. It was explained at the time that changes were being made which would improve the effectiveness of the CEPs. Some improvements have occurred, but they did not correct most of the problems of the program. And as the CEPs have become more institutionalized, reform has become more difficult, so that the only alternative is their replacement with a whole new administrative set-up, which is now being proposed.

EXTENDING A SUCCESSFUL APPROACH TO A NEW CLIENTELE

The Vocational Rehabilitation program illustrates the problem of extending a proven approach to help a different clientele. The idea of one-stop delivery and individualized service, which was central to the Concentrated Employment Program, had been applied successfully for many years under the Vocational Rehabilitation program. Serving the mentally and physically handicapped since 1920, this program provided its clients with counseling, medical care, job training, and other services deemed necessary, most of which were purchased from other agencies.

During the 1960s, the Vocational Rehabilitation program expanded rapidly as a result of widespread support and proven success. Its administrators, respectful of existing jurisdictional boundaries, were involved in few bureaucratic hassles. They maintained an especially close working relationship with the medical establishment and with the universities through research grants and training fellowships. The program has been well served by a powerful lobby, the National Rehabilitation Association, whose task has been made easier because its cause is "just." Vocational Rehabilitation serves those obviously in need of help, rather than persons who could and should be working. Few could disagree with the goal of training the mentally and physically handicapped to become self-supporting.

There is little doubt that Vocational Rehabilitation was effective in serving this clientele. In fiscal 1969, for example, 140,000 persons were "rehabilitated," or, in other words, received some form of assistance. The clients were a seriously disadvantaged group, two-thirds having less than a high school education and only a fourth being employed before enrolling in the program. Seventeen percent had orthopedic impairments, 27 percent were suffering from mental illnesses or retardation, and almost all of the others had some type of physical or mental disability. Yet those chosen for rehabilitation were "creamed" openly and without apology from the universe of an estimated 4 million physically handicapped. After an initial evaluation, only those with "reasonable prospects of success" were helped.

Assistance under Vocational Rehabilitation cost an average of $1,100 for those receiving training, and $350 for those receiving medical assistance alone. Since most services are purchased from existing agencies and institutions, the program is dependent upon the adequacy of these purchasable services. Though diagnosis and counseling accounted for a small proportion of total expenditures ($102 and $67 per case, respectively), they were essential features. Vocational rehabilitators are perhaps the most highly trained of any group of counselors, and they are well-equipped to determine the best mix of services for the client.

As a result of these relatively low expenditures per client and because applicants are creamed, rehabilitants increased their earnings many fold. In fiscal 1968, those who had averaged weekly earnings of $5.35 the week before training earned $65.00 after completion. Though these statistics inflate progress because the client may have been only temporarily out of work before joining the program, careful analysis has shown that the long-run economic and social benefits substantially exceed the costs of the program.

Because of the large numbers of physically and mentally handicapped who still cannot be served, there is little doubt that Vocational Rehabilitation could be expanded without much loss in effectiveness if staff shortages could be met. However, it is doubtful that the program will be as successful in serving a different type clientele. This has nonetheless been the assumption of legislative amendments in 1965 and 1968 which would extend coverage to the socially, economically, and educationally disadvantaged in addition to those with certified mental and physical handicaps. The Vocational Rehabilitation concept of individualized counseling and services has also been borrowed as a model for other manpower programs, again on the assumption that what works for retardees and physically handicapped will work for narcotics, the poorly motivated, and those who simply lack job skills.

The Vocational Rehabilitation establishment has shown little enthusiasm for becoming a general-purpose manpower agency. In

11

1965, socioeconomic handicaps were added to the definition of mental disabilities, so that the disadvantaged could have been served under the program. The 1968 legislation authorized a program expressly for this group, to evaluate their work potential and to prescribe the services they would need. But appropriations have not been actively sought for this authority, nor have they been received. Almost all rehabilitants are still those suffering from certified mental and physical difficulties. Vocational rehabilitators generally feel that their mission is to serve this group, and their ties with the medical establishment are an obstacle to seeking clients not included in the jurisdiction of physicians. Vocational Rehabilitation administrators are also reluctant to step on any toes in the manpower field. There is little chance that the expertise of these rehabilitators will be used for the socioeconomically disadvantaged, and there must be some doubt that the methods of the program can succeed for this clientele without experienced and highly trained counselors.

Where one-stop delivery and individualized services have been offered to the disadvantaged, as under CEP and WIN, success has been far less than under Vocational Rehabilitation. This might reflect the fact that the rehabilitators, as a rule, are more highly skilled at this type of work than the manpower employees under their newer programs. Individualized attention is not very productive if the counselors do not know what they are about and cannot suggest the best package of services for their clients. This approach is also of little use if, because of frictions with other agencies, the full range of services which may be needed by the clientele is not available. The Vocational Rehabilitation program had excellent relations nurtured over the years; new efforts will not have these contacts. On the other hand, prescribing solutions for those with social and economic disabilities may be much more difficult than determining the needs of the mentally and physically handicapped. An artificial limb can be provided for an amputee, but the treatment for low motivation remains elusive. Likewise, getting a job paying the minimum wage for a crippled man may be an achievement, while for a ghetto youth it may be an insult.

THE PROPER VEHICLE FOR A CONCEPT

The conceptual attractiveness of an idea does not necessarily mean that the notion can be transformed into an action program or that a manpower agency is the proper vehicle for its implementation of the proposal. Perhaps the most dismal failure to date among all the manpower and related efforts has been the Special Impact Program (SIP). Sponsored by Senators Jacob K. Javits and Robert F. Kennedy, the measure was initiated by amendment to the Economic Opportunity Act in 1966. Its broadly stated aim was the economic development of urban ghettos through the concentration of private and public resources. In the first year of operations, the bulk of funds were transferred to the Concentrated Employment Program, but Congress made it clear that Special Impact was thereafter to be used to assist efforts to bring or develop jobs and businesses in the ghetto. Its model was the Bedford-Stuyvesant Restoration Corporation which had been supported with an initial $7 million of the first $25 million Special Impact appropriation.

Economic development efforts in Bedford-Stuyvesant were carefully conceived, though some observers have questioned the specific steps taken to implement the idea. Special Impact funded two sister corporations, one community controlled, holding ultimate power over decisions, and the other made up of noted leaders in public life, including Senators Javits and Kennedy and IBM's President Thomas Watson. The cooperation of businessmen was sought in developing new firms and attracting branch plants of outside firms. The most notable success was the establishment of an IBM branch plant which eventually employed some 400 Bedford-Stuyvesant residents, located in the ghetto as a direct result of Thomas Watson's personal commitment. But a variety of smaller businesses were also developed through technical assistance, loans, and jawboning. Though the cost per job developed was high, the effort was judged to be relatively successful in its first year. This success would not have been possible without the active involvement of Senators Javits and Kennedy and the work of a number of business luminaries. There was little likelihood that this experience could be replicated elsewhere.

More typical was the Hough Development Corporation, also funded under Special Impact, though directly from OEO. This community group in Cleveland, formed in 1967, had more community support than the Bedford-Stuyvesant efforts but lacked its business connections. The focus was therefore on developing businesses to be run by indigenous minority entrepreneurs. The projects included a rubber-molding plant, a contractor's loan-guarantee, and a shopping-housing complex. Though some would dispute the success of the Hough effort, whatever achievements it had were due largely to the nature and style of its leadership. The charismatic head of the corporation pulled together disparate community factions and gained some influence among Cleveland businessmen. Unfortunately, charisma is a commodity in short supply elsewhere, especially in combination with competency.

OEO funded some 13 other community development corporations which plunged into the support of community capitalism based on the claimed initial success in Bedford-Stuyvesant and Hough. These other projects were generally unsuccessful because of meager business support, inadequate leadership, or both.

A recognized problem was the lack of financial incentives to attract larger businesses to the ghetto. As a solution, a broadly bipartisan group introduced the Community Self-Determination Bill in the 90th Congress to create a new, locally-controlled institution, the Community Development Corporation (CDC). With special tax privileges, which would be extended to firms opening branch plants in the area, these CDCs could, it was hoped, attract some larger businesses. Support for this bill almost disappeared in the 91st Congress, when the shortcomings of some of the existing efforts were revealed and the idea of community control lost much of its popularity. There were many theoretical drawbacks, and the CDC approach required testing before large-scale implementation. What Hough, Bedford-Stuyvesant, and other development groups showed was that with limited funds, only smaller business could be attracted or developed, and that the price was high. It is still not known whether federal support of community capitalism is workable, especially whether it could have been more effective with more intensive assistance.

A way of bypassing community groups in developing ghetto economies was to deal directly with new or expanding firms, and this was the alternative course followed by the Labor Department using its delegated funds under SIP. By 1970, nearly $17 million had been obligated through contracts with private firms to locate in or near urban ghettos, ten of these in Los Angeles and nine in New York. Under the contracts, employers received subsidies for each disadvantaged person hired, with federal funds covering the higher costs of setting up and operating ghetto plants and hiring these persons. For instance, the ten firms in Los Angeles were to receive a total of $8.9 million for hiring a minimum of 3,750 disadvantaged persons.

As subsequent evaluations funded by the Labor Department have shown, this effort was undermined by poor administration. The Department of Labor had no competence in supporting economic development efforts. Its contracts were let without broad solicitation, and in the case of Los Angeles, all of them resulted from contacts with a single investment firm which turned on the federal spigots, at a healthy fee, for new or marginal firms with financial problems. Standards were loose in selecting contractors and in writing their contracts; the apparent criterion for the subsidy level was the amount of need, while the financial stability of the contractors was given little consideration in their choice. Government interests were not protected, since the firms could get subsidies even if they hired no workers, and since plant locations were loosely stipulated. Several of the firms chose sites which were some distance from the nearest ghetto. All of these poor management practices resulted from the attempt to distribute SIP funds as quickly as possible, and also because of the reliance on a single investment counselor to arrange most of the transactions. Several firms dropped their contracts; others went bankrupt; few hired their quotas of disadvantaged workers. In early 1970, the administration of SIP funds was transferred back to OEO.

SIP offered no real test of locational subsidies; it merely demonstrated the effects of slipshod management. But as a result of these experiences, and of those with the community development corporations, it was concluded that neither approach would work. Emphasis was shifted to insuring the risks inherent in ghetto operations rather than providing locational subsidies or working through local groups. Because the programs which were undertaken to test these earlier concepts were poorly designed and implemented, with unfavorable results, these were abandoned, even though either might have worked with more forethought and better administration.

PROGRAMS AS SOCIAL EXPERIMENTS

Because of the many factors which can affect the operation of a program, evaluations of its performance, no matter how adequate, will not provide unequivocal answers about the effectiveness of underlying approaches. Success does not insure that a program can be expanded or replicated under other circumstances. Where an approach works for one clientele, it may not work for another. And if a program fails, the shortcomings in implementation or the peculiar problems it may have faced must be considered; if these are correctable and the clear cause of failure, the approach has to be retested.

These factors have not always been given adequate consideration. Success in the case of Jobs Now had to be discounted by the singular ingredients of its performance and the very obvious question about their replicability elsewhere. The constraints on extension and expansion were not weighed carefully enough, and the result was the very doubtful performance of many CEPs. Gradual expansion, with more careful choice of locations, would have resulted in far less waste and far greater success. Of course, hindsight is better than foresight, and replicability factors are difficult to isolate, but more consideration should have been given to them.

The Vocational Rehabilitation approach, which was highly effective in serving those with mental and physical handicaps, was assumed by Congress to be equally applicable to the disadvantaged without such handicaps. The attempt to alter the focus of the Vocational Rehabilitation program increasingly to serve this group was resisted by those who felt it should continue to operate in proved ways.

The failures of community development corporations and locational subsidies under SIP led to the abandonment or de-emphasis of both approaches. The community development groups could not have much impact because they lacked the resources to attract large employers to the ghetto, and the subsidies for employers were so poorly administered that little could be learned. There is no real way of knowing the potential of these approaches.

In all the illustrations, the rapid pace of implementation was a major cause of difficulties. The poor administration of the SIP effort by the Labor Department was due to the fact that proposals were demanded immediately and funds were there to spend even though guidelines were not clearly drawn. CEP's expansion to other cities occurred under the threat of urban violence and again was too rapid to allow careful deliberation about program operations and directions.

Clearly, then, the success or failure of a program does not testify to the soundness or shortcomings of its underlying assumptions. The lessons from the manpower programs should be used with caution. So many factors determine program performance that final judgments about the scope and direction of any given effort should not be based upon a few observations.

On the other hand, it is wrong to disregard the measured performance of projects and especially to expand approaches which have no record of success. When the CEPs were serving 22 areas in 1968, there was general recognition that their effectiveness was limited. Nonetheless, they were expanded in the next year in the belief that changes which had been made would improve their performance and hopefully prevent riots. The riots did not occur, and in retrospect it can be concluded that CEP should have been tested before expansion.

17

If the variables which underlie performance are given careful consideration, the programs can serve as reasonably good experiments. Under most programs, this has been the case. Administrators have usually responded to evidence produced through measurement and evaluation, but were frequently obliged to base their decisions on other factors which they found more persuasive and controlling. Administrative and legislative actions are never made in a vacuum, and program performance depends on many variables and exogenous factors which cannot be controlled.

3

Measuring and Evaluating Performance

THE RHETORIC: The performance of the manpower programs can be measured and evaluated.

THE REALITY: Because of inadequate data and limitations in the evaluative techniques, it is difficult to compare the effectiveness of the programs and approaches.

All manpower programs have been subjected to measurement and evaluation, though there is wide variation in the scope and accuracy of these investigations. A number of useful insights have resulted, and it is only as a consequence of measurement and evaluation that the programs can be meaningfully discussed. Unfortunately, data are too often inadequate and the analytical techniques limited. These limitations are not always apparent because more information is available under manpower programs than elsewhere, and because the methods of analysis are complex and somewhat of a mystic art to the uninitiated. Those on the outside and those who are being persuaded are often left with an inflated impression about the effectiveness of measurement and evaluation. Their shortcomings should be clearly spelled out by those who are cognizant of the uses and limitations of available data.

At first glance, it is deceivingly simple to measure and compare the effectiveness of the manpower programs. Enrollees benefit from services aimed at increasing their employability and earnings, so improvements can be translated into dollars-and-cents terms. Post-enrollment earnings can be compared with those before participation or else with the experience of a control group of non-participants having similar characteristics. Measured differentials can then be projected into the future, and their present value weighed against costs. The degree to which the value of benefits exceeds the costs is an indication of the return on investment in a given program. Rates of return can be compared for different approaches, with a higher rate suggesting a more worthwhile public investment.

The above is, of course, a crude outline of cost-benefit analysis. Economists have sold the technique as a major tool for evaluating manpower programs. Almost all manpower programs have been subjected to cost-benefit studies ranging widely in their detail and sophistication. Despite its widespread use, however, this technique disguises many complexities, and many of its applications are of doubtful reliability and usefulness. The data needed for such analyses are usually unavailable, so that refined analytical structures must be built on suspect empirical foundations. Within the analytical structures, many assumptions must be made which can drastically affect the outcome of analysis and yet they are hidden from all but the most careful scrutiny. In addition, there is little agreement about the meaning of any particular cost-benefit figure, and different interpretations can lead to markedly different prescriptions. These problems of measuring and evaluating program performance with the cost-benefit technique are well illustrated by a worthy attempt to analyze the effectiveness of the Job Corps.

A CASE STUDY OF COST-BENEFIT ANALYSIS

The Job Corps was launched under the Economic Opportunity Act of 1964 to provide vocational and basic education to youths in a residential setting, under the assumption that removal from

20

debilitating home environments would be necessary for training to be effective. Two types of centers were available for men in the initial years of the program. Those most deficient in preparation for work were placed in rural centers where the emphasis was on basic education combined with conservation work; those with better education received intensive vocational training in urban centers. For women, centers were opened in smaller urban areas; these emphasized training for clerical and service positions with fewer educational offerings, since women, as a rule, had more schooling than the men. Job Corps costs were high—almost $8,000 per enrollee each year—because of the living expenses involved in residential training, because of the intensive services which were offered, and because of the severely disadvantaged clientele which was being served.

In 1966, OEO sponsored a cost-benefit study to determine whether the impact of the Job Corps on enrollees justified this substantial investment. The study considered two sets of data: educational gains of enrollees and improvements in earnings after leaving Job Corps centers. Since educational levels are closely correlated with lifetime earnings, it was assumed that educational gains in the Job Corps could be used as a basis for predicting future income improvements. Initial Job Corps data indicated that after nine months in a center, the average corpsman increased his scores on achievement tests by 1.6 years of schooling. It was assumed that this measured permanent educational gain would result in greater lifetime earnings.

Hourly earnings data were available for corpsmen and for a control group of "no-shows"—youths accepted for enrollment who had not participated. Comparison showed that the weighted average hourly wage gain of corpsmen exceeded that of "no-shows" by 12 cents an hour when measured after both groups had been in the labor force six months. Projection of this differential over a lifetime was recognizedly dubious, but it gave another estimate of increased lifetime earnings as a result of the Job Corps experience.

Relying upon these two sets of data, the OEO study concluded that the "realistic" ratio of benefits over costs was 1.22, ranging

21

from 1.05 to 1.69, depending upon a variety of assumptions made. This was interpreted to mean that for every dollar invested in the Job Corps, the rate of return was 22 percent, making it a "worthwhile" investment of government funds.

Subsequent data, far different from those used in the study, yielded a much less optimistic picture. On the one hand, claims that enrollees gained 1.6 years of schooling for every nine months in the Corps were clearly inflated. Later estimates were less than half of those asserted earlier. Since the benefits were calculated by a formula which was linearly related to educational gains, the newer figures meant that the cost-benefit ratio would be cut in half. Job Corps spokesmen claimed that the later and more complete data were subject to errors, and to no one's surprise, they were never released officially by the agency, although they were published by a private source. Careful examination of the arguments suggests that while these estimates may have been low, the earlier ones were definitely high. In other words, on the basis of widely varying estimates of educational gains, the Job Corps benefit-cost ratio might range from 1.69 to .53, permitting the conclusion that the Corps could be either a fairly worthwhile investment or a waste of money.

The data on earnings and employment used in the second set of cost-benefit calculations also provide a questionable basis for analysis. Taken after six months' exposure to the labor market, they differed markedly from 12- and 18-month follow-up data. The later data indicated increasing unemployment among former corpsmen, with the rate for dropouts falling while that for graduates rose. Average hourly wage differentials also declined between graduates and dropouts, though there were no follow-up surveys of "noshows." Obviously, projections of the six months' experience inflated estimates of lifetime benefits. With time the differential gains of Job Corps participants apparently eroded, though it is difficult to measure this with any precision because of declining sample sizes as fewer and fewer persons were traced in each of the subsequent follow-up attempts.

At the time the study was made, no other data were available to estimate the effectiveness of the Job Corps, and there was no reason to assume that those which were used were fraught with error. In retrospect, any use of these data on educational gains, or improvements in employment and earnings, should have been suspect. There is little doubt that the actual benefit-cost ratios calculated from these data were too high.

A less obvious source of bias was the set of assumptions made in calculating benefits and costs from these data. For instance, payments for clothing, subsistence, and allowances, running to almost $2,000 per enrollee each year, were excluded on the reasoning that they did not involve any net increase in resource use since they would have been provided anyway. From society's point of view, this is true, but in measuring the return of the program relative to one providing nonresidential training, it is invalid. Including these, thereby increasing costs by more than a fourth, would reduce the benefit-cost ratio by the same amount. The arguments for inclusion and exclusion both carry weight, and the decision is arbitrary, but either has a crucial effect on the results.

Assumptions must also be made in calculating benefits, especially in projecting into the future and discounting back to the present. Any projection introduces a large element of uncertainty. The use of educational gains data was meant to circumvent this problem, since educational attainment is closely correlated with lifetime earnings; but the current relationship between earnings and education may not prevail in the future. Can we, for example, say that a person achieving a grade more education will earn the same differential income 40 years from now as a person who was educated 40 years ago? Also, those who made it the first time around may be inherently higher achievers than corpsmen and more likely to have brighter employment prospects.

The discounting problem is equally perplexing. Future benefits, translated into dollars-and-cents terms, have a present value which is less than their absolute amount, and this depends on the interest rate just the same as the present value of a bond payable at some later date. The assumptions made about the discounting rates are crucial. For instance, the Job Corps benefit-cost ratios were calculated for two alternative discount rates, 3 and 5 percent. At the 3 percent rate, the benefit-cost ratio under one set of assumptions was 1.22 to 1.00, while at the 5 percent rate the comparable ratio was only .79 to 1.00. Obviously, the choice of discount rate can make a difference whether the program is judged worthwhile or a waste. In comparing programs, the choice is important even if the same factor is used in analyzing both. Programs with a longer-run payoff will have a relatively higher cost-benefit ratio compared with shorter-run programs if the discount factor is small. For instance, a basic education program might seem more effective than a simple placement program at a 3 percent discount rate, but less effective if a 5 percent rate is assumed.

To compound all these problems, cost-benefit ratios are particularly susceptible to misuse. With all their critical assumptions and inherent data problems, cost-benefit studies usually end up producing a range of ratios among which one is considered more probable or most suitable for public consumption. Office of Economic Opportunity officials, including its top research personnel (who might have been expected to know better), used the Job Corps' 1.22 benefit-cost ratio as "proof" of its effectiveness, claiming that the program was returning 22 percent on the social investment. A different ratio could just as plausibly be calculated from the same data which would indicate no return, and even this would mean little without comparative measures for alternative approaches serving the clientele. In that case, questions about discount rates and other assumptions would become critical, and the ratios alone could not be used.

LIMITATIONS OF MEASUREMENT AND EVALUATION

Despite its many problems, the Job Corps benefit-cost study was one of the best applications of this technique to manpower programs. It can hardly be claimed, therefore, that benefit-cost analysis made much of a substantive contribution to measuring the impact of manpower programs. Its use was mainly political, offering "scientific" support or opposition to the funding of manpower programs. There are many inherent limitations to this approach.

Most basically, the data needed for refined cost-benefit analysis are rarely available. Records of pre-enrollment and post-enrollment experiences or of the services which are offered to particular enrollees are skimpy. Follow-up data are usually gathered through surveys which too often cover only a minute portion of those who have been served. As in the case of the Job Corps, follow-up data become more and more "iffy" the longer the period they cover, which is rarely long enough to get a firm basis for predicting the future impact. There may also be an increasing "non-response bias," if either the more or less successful enrollees have a higher probability of not being traced.

However, competent and carefully designed samples can provide much useful information where there have been no institutional arrangements for follow-up. The Louis Harris Job Corps studies were pioneer efforts of this type dealing with manpower programs. Currently, a variety of follow-up surveys are being undertaken, though many are too piecemeal or small-scale to be useful. One promising area is a major comparative study by the Operations Research Corporation of the post-enrollment experience by participants in MDTA-institutional, NYC out-of-school, JOBS (only those under contract), and the Job Corps programs.

One of the most severe problems is the lack of control group data. Operational program statistics are concerned with those who are served and not with those outside the program. Control groups usually have to be selected for each study and carefully sampled. Selection is easier said than done. Demographic characteristics can usually be matched, but there is a wide margin for difference within these statistics. If, as is often claimed, the programs "cream" from the available clientele—for instance, picking the most highly motivated among 18-year-old black youths from families on welfare—the performance of enrollees might be quite different from that of the cohort. The use of "no-shows" (applicants selected for a program but who did not participate) as a control group gets around this problem in some ways, but introduces other possible biases relating to their reasons for not participating in the programs. It is easy to slough these off as technical factors, but they can have a significant impact on the comparative measures and final results of any follow-up study.

Even if adequate data were available, cost-benefit analyses of different programs would vary in their assumptions and techniques, so that their calculated ratios would not be strictly comparable. This is especially the case when different groups are being served. For instance, several cost-benefit studies have been made of MDTA, another remedial training program, suggesting that its rate of return is substantially higher than that of the Job Corps. Cost-benefit ratios for Vocational Rehabilitation are apparently even larger. This, however, does not necessarily justify a transfer of resources from the Job Corps to Vocational Rehabilitation and MDTA. The programs are not substitutes, since they focus on different segments of the population. The Job Corps serves the most seriously disadvantaged clientele of any manpower program; Vocational Rehabilitation devotes most of its attention to the physically handicapped; and MDT counts among its clients many with stable labor force attachment who may have been displaced by technological changes or overall economic decline in their communities. Shifting emphasis among programs means shifting emphasis among these clients. Most likely, manpower programs would achieve higher benefit-cost ratios if they would serve only high school graduates. No sophisticated or complicated analysis is needed to prove that the cost to train those with the most serious problems is higher, while the measurable benefits in terms of increased potential earnings per dollar invested may be lower than for clients who need little remedial help.

The shortcomings of measurement and evaluation lie deeper than the lack of adequate data and the limitations of analytical techniques. A basic problem is that measurement and evaluation are often focused on variables which do not lend themselves to improve program effectiveness. What data are available and what conclusions have been drawn do not answer many of the vital questions which are basic to the design and mix of programs. In simplest terms, emphasis has been on the form of programs rather than their substance. Almost every program consists of a group of services; for instance, the Job Corps offers enrollees counseling, health care, food and shelter, vocational training, basic education, work experience, placement assistance, and much more. Little effort has been exerted to discover which of these may or may not be important, and more specifically, which services, and in what doses, are most useful to any particular type of enrollee. The usual data consist of average enrollee characteristics, average per person costs for each type of service or group of services, and average gains in employment and earnings as a result of the package of services. Few longitudinal studies have been funded to trace individuals through the system and thereby permit more refined analysis of the effect of different approaches on different groups of enrollees. Manpower administrators are aware of this need, but longitudinal studies are expensive and by definition their results will not be available for years. Administrators rarely have the luxury of postponing decisions that long while awaiting the returns from research projects. Nonetheless, the Department of Labor has funded a large-scale longitudinal study of various labor force groups, which is a laudable step, but similar data are needed tracing participants through each of the manpower programs.

Evaluators as well as data collectors are to blame for the failures of measurement and evaluation. They have seldom made the fullest use of available data to improve understanding of these matters. Most research has covered specific programs. Usually it is funded by the administrative agency which is seeking to justify expansion or at least to secure continued funding and is concerned, at best, with the program's overall impact. While some manpower experts have encompassed almost all the programs in the course of their studies, their observations about underlying approaches have rarely extended across program boundaries. The emphasis has too often been on the differences among legislative origins, program offerings, funding, and clienteles, rather than on the similarities between programs. This is understandable because

27

of the lack of carrots to stimulate research on alternative services which may be offered under several different efforts.

In the few cases where the more difficult road has been taken and where the assumptions and approaches have been tested, some surprising results have come to light. For instance, one of the sacred cows of manpower programs is that counseling is of major assistance. This assumption was tested by a New York City project which provided counseling to vocational high school girls. The hypothesis to be tested was that four years of concentrated attention from professional social service workers would result in constructive behaviorial changes. This was not, in fact, the case. There was little difference between the social histories of those girls who were counseled and the experiences of a control group who were left to their own devices.

This was a very simple test because of the single-service, single-purpose design of the program. In manpower programs it is more difficult to isolate the impact of a single service. In the Job Corps, for example, the effects of counseling, whatever they may be, are not easily isolated from the effects of other services. But there is no *a priori* reason to believe that counseling should be expanded or even that it is worthwhile; this should be subjected to test. Similarly, appraisals of the Job Corps and of other programs should try to discern the value of each of the major component services they offer, and how they are best provided.

To develop the data needed to form judgments about the impact of an individual service is a difficult but not impossible task. For instance, the necessary measurements could have been developed in Job Corps centers where the control over participants is greater than in other programs, and the different combinations of services being offered at the different types of centers provided a laboratory for testing their effectiveness. A promising and concise area of study would have been to test the importance of residency in the success of the Job Corps. The feeding and housing of enrollees involves considerable costs to the government, but since the widely held belief was that youths had to be removed from their debilitating home environments in order to benefit from train-

28

ing, the Job Corps has amassed little solid evidence to examine the impact of residency. Though four small experimental centers were opened in cities which provided Job Corps training to a regular clientele but on a nonresidential basis, all withered away without adequately testing the assumption that residency is an essential ingredient to achieve the goals of the program. While costs per trainee were substantially lower in these centers, it was found that absenteeism was a massive problem, and consequently educational gains were limited. The tentative conclusion of these experiments would seem to be that getting away from home is helpful to the average teenage youth from a seriously disadvantaged family. Nevertheless, when the Job Corps was cut back and restructured under the new administration, and urban centers with nonresident facilities were planned, the implication was that residency was of doubtful significance despite the limited evidence to the contrary.

Obviously, it is important to analyze the separate approaches of the programs to test as much as possible their underlying assumptions. Data must be generated which will make this possible, and funds for evaluation must be provided outside the administrative framework of specific programs.

There is also a dearth of research providing insights into institutional and other ingredients to success. The wide variation of failure and success among projects at the state and local level is too often ignored because the variability is disguised in the aggregation of statistics.

The major effort to provide a comparative perspective of local diversity has been a careful investigation of the total impact of manpower programs in four cities, prepared by the Olympus Research Corporation. It sought to determine the ingredients of success or failure based on local variations in program design, administration, clientele, and operating environment. This worm's-eye view is vastly different from the bird's-eye perspective, and it provides many valuable insights.

There has been a disproportionate emphasis on the evaluation of aggregate and national program performance. While this may have been justified as using scarce resources most effectively, more attention to developments at the state and local levels is now needed in order to estimate the replicability of successful approaches and to help communities benefit from the mistakes of others. The demand for information about state and local administration is likely to be intensified if manpower programs are decentralized. Higher priority should be given to comparative case studies of manpower efforts in different areas.

THE CONTRIBUTIONS OF MEASUREMENT AND EVALUATION

Despite these numerous shortcomings, careful data collection and refined analysis contribute to rational decision-making. Where cost-benefit evaluations are carefully used, with appreciation of the technique's limitations, more informed judgments can result. For instance, the Job Corps cost-benefit analysis suggested that the high investment per enrollee was not wasted, and that discounted benefits were reasonable and within the same ballpark. The cost-benefit technique provided a useful framework for evaluating the Job Corps —as contrasted with the popular Congressional exercise of comparing the price of a Harvard education with Job Corps costs. It focused on the real policy issues, while the Harvard-Job Corps comparisons were a futile exercise and attempted to compare entirely unrelated outlays serving different populations. The cost-benefit approach reminds those who use the tool that in measuring the effectiveness of any investment, the rate of return is of major importance and not the amount of outlay alone. It highlights the point that benefits and costs cannot be considered separately.

Cost-benefit analysis also provides a framework which can be used to evaluate the performance of similar projects under different circumstances. For instance, the Job Corps analysis revealed that there was a wide variation in performance between the types of centers, suggesting that reform was needed and also indicating that the urban centers were probably a better investment, despite their higher costs per enrollee, than rural conservation centers. This called for further internal investigations into the reasons for suc-

30

cess or failure and also for administrative changes. Cost-benefit analysis helped to focus attention on the problems needing solution. The value of this contribution should not be underrated.

The application of data collected under the manpower programs to cost-benefit analysis is perhaps their least significant use. Manpower data have yielded insights into program content and achievements, increasing the rationality of legislative and administrative decisions. Most significantly, they have made possible a wide range of evaluations which have led to improvements in program performance. It is laudable that most of the information which has been generated is well-distributed, and certainly this is essential if it is to have an impact on policy. Some further steps could be taken in this direction, especially in strengthening data collection and research at the local level, but a wealth of information is available for those who want it. These data will not supply easy answers to the questions raised about the effectiveness of programs, but they can help policy shapers and program administrators to make educated guesses and base their decisions on informed opinion rather than whim. In the final analysis, as Henry Clay put it, "statistics are no substitute for judgment," but rational decision-making is well served when judgment is based upon statistics.

4

Applying the Lessons Learned

THE RHETORIC: Measurement and evaluation have had a significant impact on the design and mix of programs.

THE REALITY: The lessons of social experimentation have often
been ignored, giving place to more "political" considerations.

Within and between programs, there have been significant changes
in emphasis and approach. Since most of the manpower tools
were new, they had to be honed down, their uses defined, and their
application improved. In the process, their effectiveness was probably increased. The issue is the extent to which improvements under the manpower programs were the products of conscious measurement and evaluation or whether the improvements would have
taken place in the absence of the "experimental" efforts. Did measurement and evaluation have an important influence on the design and administration of the manpower programs? The answer
to this question is difficult because the forces that gave impetus to
program changes are complex and cannot be subjected to meaningful regression analysis measuring the separate impact of evalu-

ation. However, the experience of the four major programs—the Neighborhood Youth Corps, the Job Corps, MDTA, and Vocational Education—suggests that experimental feedback has played some role in indicating the needs for improvement, but has had all too little impact on the changes made in response to these needs.

RATIONALE FOR CHANGE UNDER NYC

The Neighborhood Youth Corps (NYC) was designed as a work experience, income maintenance, and training program for youths. There are three types of operations. Part-time jobs are provided for those in school, under the assumption that extra income will forestall dropouts for economic reasons. Summer NYC employs youths who might otherwise be "on the streets," the aim being to cushion their return to school the next fall. For out-of-school youths, NYC provides jobs and training, but most of all income, during the years of least employability.

Changes in emphasis among these components have been significant, but have not been based on evaluations of underlying concepts and program performance. Summer NYC has expanded, becoming NYC's largest component. Each year, expansion has been accepted under the very real threat that high levels of summer youth unemployment will lead to unrest in the cities. It has never been demonstrated that summer NYC increases the likelihood of return to school, that the work experience is particularly useful in later life, nor, in fact, that it buys urban peace, though certainly urban unrest has eased. Instead, growth has been fostered by a crisis atmosphere, with little attention to improving the employability or education of enrollees.

In-school enrollments reached their peak in fiscal 1966 and since then have been declining. Earlier studies indicate that dropout rates were significantly reduced by participation in the program, and that its impact was favorable. More recent analysis has concluded that this positive appraisal resulted from the "creaming" which had occurred in selecting those who were least likely to

33

drop out anyway. For comparable groups, dropout rates were apparently not improved, although one major study concluded that former NYC enrollees had a better employment and earnings record than a control group. The case in either direction is not clearcut. Nevertheless, the positive aspects were emphasized when the program was new and politically popular, whereas the negative side was emphasized when it lost some of its glamor. The conclusiveness in either direction was not enough to justify program changes, even though the rise and subsequent decline in enrollments were claimed to be based on careful analysis.

Finally, enrollments in out-of-school NYC have been cut more drastically, by almost a half over the last four years. Evaluations of post-enrollment experience found that there was no noticeable improvement in the earnings or employment rates of participants, and these negative findings had much to do with the program's de-emphasis. Here was a case where evaluation led directly to change aimed at improving performance. Recently, emphasis has shifted within the program to more intensive education and training, increased expenditures per enrollee, and lighter workloads. These enriched services are expected to improve the long-range employability of participants. But there is no proof as yet that more intensive services will help enrollees enough to justify their costs, especially considering the very short average length of stay. Measurement and evaluation will have to continue until the performance can be assessed. More intensive services under NYC are an extension of the experiment to help out-of-school youths; they are not a solution based on experimentation. Thus, analysis has pointed out the areas where improvement is needed but has not proved how this can be accomplished.

CHANGE FOR CHANGE'S SAKE

Another example of dubious social experimentation is the checkered history of the Job Corps. In its more controversial days, Job Corps appropriations seemed to receive more Congressional attention than the entire defense budget. Pages of the *Congressional Record* were filled with comparisons between Job Corps costs and those of a Harvard education. This is a program which was literally publicized to death, with overemphasis of every failure or success.

As indicated earlier, careful analysis of the post-enrollment experience of corpsmen and women revealed improvements in employment and earnings. There is little disagreement that improvements did occur, though these may have been exaggerated at times and though the evidence is inconclusive whether the advantage of former enrollees may fade out after a while. The issue was whether these justified the very high costs of residential training, which averaged annually nearly $8,000 per slot in the early years of the program. Calculations of costs and benefits generally concluded that the higher expenditures were worthwhile but that the variations of effectiveness among the centers and types of centers were large. Elimination of the least effective centers was clearly needed to improve the overall performance of the program.

Coming into office with the promise that it would end the waste in the Job Corps, the Nixon administration did more than trim the fat off of the program; it closed 59 of 123 centers. A careful procedure was set up to insure that the least effective centers were closed, and a variety of performance factors were considered and then weighed. Whatever the objectivity of the initial assessments of performance, the weighting was slanted toward reducing costs. The proportional impact of subsequent closings on the different types of centers was contrary to some evidence of their relative cost-effectiveness. Enrollments in urban centers were cut the most drastically, though their performance was relatively better than either men's rural centers or women's centers. The explanation for the relative reductions could not be found in the comparative effectiveness of the different types of centers, but in Congressional policy declarations and preferences. The conservation centers, by most measures, were the least effective, despite their lower cost and considering their more disadvantaged clientele. Perhaps in recognition of the strength of conservation interests and the requirements of the law, they were reduced proportionately less than

35

the other types. Urban centers with large nonresident enrollment were to be opened in place of many of the closed centers despite the doubtful record of experimental nonresidential centers, which experienced high dropout and absentee rates. Subsequently, nonresidential training has made little headway; only a few new urban centers were opened and few of their trainees were commuters. But the original decision was made on political as much as analytical grounds, though the action was claimed to be based on refined analysis of performance.

In with the New, Out with the Old

Perhaps the most successful example of "experimental engineering" has been MDTA, initiated under the Manpower Development and Training Act of 1962 to retrain stable workers whose skills had become obsolete due to changes in technology. With improving economic conditions, most of MDTA's intended clientele found employers competing for their services without added publicly supported training. MDTA was redirected to serve a greater percentage of disadvantaged workers—those who had never held stable jobs, who had limited education and skill, and who were often the victims of discrimination in hiring. To accommodate to the more serious problems of this clientele, training allowances were extended and educational components were strengthened.

From analysis of program data and careful observation of results, further improvements were suggested and implemented. On-the-job, as opposed to institutional, training was given increasing emphasis on the basis of OJT's lower federal costs per enrollee and evidence that the post-enrollment work experience of these trainees was better than of institutional enrollees, though the OJT trainees were more qualified to begin with. As the more seriously disadvantaged were helped, OJT was coupled with institutional training to provide the basic education needed by many enrollees before they could be trained on the job site. Changes were also made in allowances to provide incentives for completers, and other improvements were carried out as their need became clear. These had broad bipartisan support, and were based on fairly concrete evidence of the need for and the directions of change.

The MDTA program benefited from a relatively experienced group of administrators. The OJT segment was run by the Bureau of Apprenticeship and Training within the Department of Labor, and vocational educators in HEW's Office of Education were in charge of institutional training. Both had been providing similar services prior to MDTA and were comparatively well-equipped to launch it in the right directions. The program also benefited from reporting and data collection procedures which were initiated early in the game and were superior to those of most other programs. Though still inadequate, these data were the basis of evaluations showing that MDTA was having a substantial impact, improving the employability and earnings of its clientele.

The reward for this success was a reduction in program levels, with a shift in resources to other efforts. In fiscal 1967, 126,000 institutional and 145,000 OJT slots were available. By fiscal 1969, despite stable annual appropriations, there were 98,000 and 68,000 slots, respectively, because MDT funds were diverted to the Concentrated Employment Program and the Job Opportunities in the Business Sector program. Institutional enrollments have leveled off at 50,000, while those in OJT have continued to decline. It is obvious that two OJT programs cannot coexist where one makes a far more attractive offer to employers, and in this case JOBS offers larger subsidies with only minimal monitoring of projects. The initiation and expansion of the newer program is a story in itself, but in brief, it grew because of its popularity among businessmen, giving them a forum to display their social consciousness in a safe, subsidized, and highly visible way. The political appeal of JOBS is the major reason it has gained pre-eminence. The unfortunate reality is that the program has not proven its worth despite its initial unsubstantiated claims of success, yet it is replacing MDTA-OJT which has demonstrated its effectiveness in serving a less disadvantaged clientele. JOBS is more costly, but it has not been shown that the training provided justifies the higher subsidies to employers.

Twixt the Cup and the Lip

The needed reforms of the Vocational Education program have long been obvious and the object of federal efforts, but they have proven extremely difficult to put into practice. In 1963 a panel of consultants, established by President Kennedy, noted a number of significant shortcomings: the paucity of data, the low quality of services, the lack of coordination with other agencies, the absence of long-range planning, an inadequacy of funds relative to needs, and a failure to adjust to changing labor market conditions. The recommendations of this panel led directly to the passage of the Vocational Education Act of 1963, which expanded appropriations fourfold, setting aside funds for data collection, research, and upgrading of staff. The act also required state plans as well as improved linkages with state employment agencies. More significantly, the law extended services to those with socioeconomic handicaps who could not successfully participate in regular programs, and it provided for training in any nonprofessional skill as opposed to the traditional categories of vocational education.

Five years later when Congress reviewed the 1963 act, only minor improvements had been made, and these were definitely disappointing to the architects of the legislation. Though more disadvantaged persons were served, the special needs group for whom records were maintained still accounted for only one percent of the total enrollment. Data continued to be scarce, interagency linkages more perfunctory than substantial, and planning only minimal.

The objectives of the 1963 legislation were not met because of the permissiveness of the legislation and the intransigence of the vocational education establishment. The law permitted funds to be allocated to new areas of activity but did not restrict them to these areas; it required nominal plans but instituted no other monitoring. Without "sticks or carrots," there was little reason for vocational educators to reform their policies significantly. Only marginal improvements resulted, with the construction of some new facilities and a small decline in the proportion of students enrolled in home economics and agriculture courses. It is easy to understand why those teaching courses would not be enthusiastic about attempts to reduce enrollments in their jurisdictions, and, at best, they acquiesced to a smaller share of the growing enrollments. Where programs were working for one clientele, and more of this type were still in need of services, most states were understandably reluctant to increase funds for special groups.

In recognition of the limited progress which had been made due to the shortcomings of the 1963 legislation, the Vocational Education Act of 1968 was passed. Besides expanding funds for post- and pre-secondary vocational education, direct and full grants were provided to finance innovative measures by the states and specific areas serving the disadvantaged or to test new approaches. The matching share under programs for the socio-economically disadvantaged was increased. Planning was required, with the intent that this would be used in allocating funds, and periodic reviews and evaluations were demanded. The 1968 act provided the incentives and controls which were left out of the 1963 act.

In all likelihood, improvements will be much more rapid, but they might be limited by several factors. Legislative intents must be translated from authorizations into appropriations, and lobbying groups—and the American Vocational Association has achieved an enviable reputation—have been known to undo in the appropriation stage what they could not reverse in authorizations. The appropriations in fiscal 1970, and the proposed budget for fiscal 1971, have in fact failed to give the intended support to the innovative measures of the 1968 act, providing meager funding for planning and experimentation, for training the specially disadvantaged, and for introducing new courses. Even if the 1968 act had been implemented at the federal level as was initially intended, there is no assurance that local practices would have changed drastically or that the federal officials who are part of the vocational establishment would carry out the legislative mandate with any vigor. Certainly the new funds will be used, and states will take advantage of more favorable matching grant formulas, but there is no assurance that this will mean more than changing the names of existing projects. Without detailed reporting and persistent over-sight, neither of which is likely, vocational educators may comply with new directives more in form than in substance. Given the decentralized decisional process under the program, the overall impact of change will probably not be large.

RUSH TO JUDGMENT

Under the Work Incentive Program, which aims at reducing re-lief rolls by inducing work, welfare recipients are given remedial training and are allowed to keep $30 a month plus 30 percent of any earnings without offsetting reductions in the relief payments they receive. Along the same line, a variety of proposals have been put forward for a guaranteed income which would help the working poor as well as those on welfare. President Nixon's Fam-ily Assistance Plan, for instance, would guarantee $500 for each of the first two family members and $300 for each additional child. This basic payment would be reduced by 50 cents for every dollar of annual earnings above $720 and would boost income of the working poor who are heads of families with children.

A basic question underlying the income maintenance proposals is the degree of incentive needed to induce work effort. There is a possibility that if a basic income is provided to low-income work-ers, or to those who could work, they are likely to loaf and live off their government checks rather than finding and holding jobs. Even observers who favor income maintenance schemes usually agree that a guaranteed income would have some impact on reducing the supply of labor, giving workers some degree of choice between leisure and drudgery, depending upon the level of payments and the wages paid in available jobs. The critical issue is the extent of such adverse effects. If they are large, income guarantees could be disastrous, bloating welfare costs by putting people on the dole who could be making it on their own effort.

To help resolve this issue, the Office of Economic Opportunity funded a $5 million project in six New Jersey cities to provide a variety of income guarantees and incentives, and to measure their effect on work effort. This project was carefully designed to test popular beliefs about the work ethic among low-income family heads, and former OEO Director Donald Rumsfeld called it "possibly the most significant social-science experiment ever to take place."

As in any social experiment, there were problems in controlling exogenous variables, selecting control groups, and evaluating data. For instance, the New Jersey sites were originally chosen because there was no AFDC-UP program and unemployed male family heads had no alternative source of relief. In January 1969, however, nine months after the project was initiated, the state adopted AFDC-UP, undermining the test of income maintenance under the work incentive experiment since the state's payments were in most cases higher than the payments under the experiment. Because of confusions in data collection, there was initially no way of comparing alternative guarantee levels and incentive rates, so that the vital issue of the optimum incentives could not be resolved. However, these difficulties can be overcome or compensated for, and it is too early to judge the quality of the experiment itself, since it is designed to run for three years.

The serious problems were not in the experiment, but rather in the fact that conclusions were drawn too quickly, making the remainder of the experiment almost anticlimatic. In August 1969, when President Nixon announced his ambitious Family Assistance Plan, there was little likelihood that it would be approved by Congress, precisely because of fears that the working poor would be led astray. To marshal support in favor of the bill, the administration gave undue publicity to a preliminary analysis of findings under the experiment. In a special White House Conference, OEO's Director Rumsfeld dramatically summarized the conclusions of the study, asserting that the experiment was proof of the approach proposed by FAP. "There is no evidence," he stated, "that work effort declined among those receiving income support payments. On the contrary, there is an indication that the work effort of the participants receiving payments increased relative to the work effort of those not receiving payments. . . ."

These presumed findings, and the widely publicized announcement, were instrumental in gaining House approval of the Family Assistance Plan. The Senate Finance Committee subjected the preliminary and tentative findings of the New Jersey experiment to more careful scrutiny, utilizing an investigation by the General Accounting Office. The latter found that the available data were inadequate to permit independent evaluation, that the results were questionable because the various guarantee and incentive schemes had no measurably different effects on incentives, that many had dropped out of the sample with the initiation of AFDC-UP, and that the experimental group had more room for improvement in earnings since 11 percent were unemployed. The GAO found little basis for drawing any conclusions so early in the experiment.

OBSTACLES TO IMPROVEMENT

The examples cited suggest that experimentation and feedback of measured results have had all too little impact on design, administration, and priorities under NYC, Vocational Education, and the Job Corps. In the MDTA program, their effects were undone by subsequent changes in policy, while the carefully designed work incentive experiment was undermined by premature evaluation for advocacy purposes. Several factors contributed to these developments.

First, research tends to focus on the most controversial areas, such as the Job Corps, which may be unpopular because of bad publicity or other factors not related to the merits of the effort. Evaluation is almost completely neglected in areas where there is wide (though unsubstantiated) agreement about the validity of an approach, as in putting welfare recipients to work under WIN, paying subsidies under JOBS, and providing income maintenance under summer NYC.

Second, program evaluations are flexible and reflect the changing fortunes of their objects of study. When in-school NYC was popular, its effect on dropout rates appeared favorable; when popularity waned, the evidence was re-examined and found to be much more equivocal. It is also in the nature of political decision-making that studies which contradict prevailing policies are often ignored, while those in agreement are given publicity.

Third, the separate programs have an inertia sustained by vested interests and established obligations to clienteles; they resist diminution even in the face of negative results. The closing of Job Corps centers was met by a hail of criticism, some coming from the program's staunchest opponents who suddenly found that the centers spent money that constituent communities did not appreciate losing. This being the case, the alternative to elimination of an unsuccessful program has been to make administrative changes which are intended to give new purpose (or "image") to ongoing efforts. Out-of-school NYC was thus altered to emphasize more intensive education and training, probably a wise move but one that was made on faith alone, at the very same time the Job Corps took the opposite course and attempted to pare the average expenditure per enrollee by reducing services.

Fourth, the success of a program does not assure its expansion. Instead, the approach may be applied under different circumstances, on a different scale, or with different methods of implementation. MDTA funds were transferred to JOBS, though the latter program may not have similarly positive results. On the other hand, real, projected or advertised success may lead to the too rapid implementation of new approaches on a larger scale without evidence about their effectiveness.

Fifth, the results of experimental efforts can be misused in support of desired policies. After ten months, the Work Incentive experiment was evaluated, and even though the conclusions were extremely tentative, they were publicized as if they were well founded. The experiment itself is not at fault, nor are those who try to make ongoing evaluations; rather, the problem is with those who distort the significance of experimental findings for advocacy purposes. The lessons of experimentation must be applied with care so that the necessary qualifications and conditions are made explicit. Too often, these are forgotten in the quest for simple, hard-hitting documentation of ideas and policies.

Finally, even when legislation is designed to implement the reforms suggested by evaluation, there can be no certainty that the desired improvements will result. Bureaucracies, especially those which are decentralized, have an inertia all their own and prove amazingly intransigent to changes made at the federal level. As the example of the Vocational Education program highlights, "sticks and carrots" must be used actively and words are not enough. Even then, reforms cannot occur too quickly where powerful vested groups are (or imagine themselves) threatened. Continuing pressure must be exerted, though the opposition of vested interest groups will seek to undermine the continuity of improvement efforts.

These illustrations suggest that in the real world there are many factors which limit the application of analytical prescriptions. Reasonable men often disagree in their assessments of a given set of "facts," and certainly manpower experts are no exception. Indeed, part of their expertise has been achieved through mastering the art of equivocation, making it easy to ignore their counsel, which is frequently offered in the tradition of the Delphic oracle. In retrospect, when the wrong decisions have been made, those without responsibility often shift their outlooks, so that there appears to be a consensus that never existed for alternative and "correct" measures.

When experts have agreed—a rare occasion—they have found that walls do not tumble at the sound of their trumpets. Vested interest groups which resist change are numerous; politics plays an important role in determining whether prescriptions are implemented; and it takes a great deal of time and effort to get anything done. Rarely is there a direct cause and effect relationship between evaluative research and legislative or administrative action. More often, the impact is tangential and gradual, with the weight of evidence slowly building into a consensus for change. It is difficult to pin down the indirect effects of evaluative research, but it is naive to ignore their existence.

Evaluative research could have a much greater impact if those who work in the vineyards were willing to live dangerously and spell out their views. If evaluators would make their work more relevant to pragmatic needs, then they would have no problem in attracting the attention of legislators. But in many agencies there is a wide breach between the research and evaluation staff and the operational staff. Many evaluations never get into the hands of legislators or the public. Congress will have to nourish its own evaluative arm if it is to secure independent evaluations of the programs it initiates and funds. Prodded by Congress, the General Accounting Office has already expanded its operations in the field of manpower, and it is reasonable to expect that the GAO could develop the needed expertise to evaluate manpower programs.

5

Establishing Priorities

THE RHETORIC: Priorities are being changed to emphasize approaches of demonstrated effectiveness.

THE REALITY: New policy thrusts are based more on ideology than on analysis.

Not surprisingly, the changeover of administrations in January 1969 was accompanied by some major shifts in emphasis in the manpower efforts. These shifts were motivated by partisan principles and ideologies, and they foreshadowed more marked developments in the future.

It is a fact of political life that changes are promoted as unequivocal improvements. The priorities expressed by administrators lead to the generation of "facts" and figures showing the need for and potential of new approaches. Three major thrusts were highlighted in the 1970 *Manpower Report*, all presumably based on past experimentation and the lessons learned. Administration spokesmen have claimed or implied that the favored approaches represent the expansion of successful efforts in the past.

First, there has been an increasing emphasis on private sector participation through wider use of on-the-job training, subsidies to private employers, appeals to corporate conscience, and government-business partnership programs. This approach gained its original impetus under the Johnson administration, but its continued and increased support has stemmed from its compatibility with the cardinal Republican ideals of reducing government intervention and placing greater reliance upon the business community in solving social problems.

Second, the administration has favored the expansion of manpower services to welfare recipients on a larger scale, anticipating that the aid offered will help them return to work—"getting them off welfare and onto workfare." Also started under the Johnson administration, this approach has received major emphasis in the Nixon administration and is an integral part of his far-reaching proposal to overhaul the relief system.

Finally, more attention, if not action, is being focused on upgrading workers to raise them out of dead-end jobs and on providing meaningful opportunities in the public sector. The intent is to help those who work but cannot earn a decent income, and it manifests an increasing concern with "locked-in" working Americans who have too few opportunities to rise much above the poverty threshold. Though resources for such efforts are still limited, they are likely to increase in the future with broad bipartisan support.

The Unwieldy Partnership between Government and Business

The share of Labor Department manpower expenditures received by private employers was slated to double between fiscal 1969 and 1970. The bulk of these funds goes to participants in the JOBS program, which subsidizes the extra costs connected with the hiring, training, and retaining disadvantaged workers. Subsidies average around $3,000 per hire. Employers also participate in JOBS on a voluntary basis, pledging jobs which they will try to fill with those who would normally be judged deficient. So far, three-fourths of the pledged slots have involved no remuneration.

In this sense, JOBS is a "partnership" program, with the government providing funds in some cases while business does the hiring and training, as well as the promotional organization work, through the National Alliance of Businessmen (NAB).

The benefits of private sector participation are obvious. Where jobs are offered to disadvantaged workers without subsidy, the aims of manpower policy are achieved at little cost. To the degree that the business sector knows its own needs and is most skilled in preparing workers to meet these needs, the training it provides will be more efficient. With "hiring first and training later," jobs are assured to participants, creating a built-in incentive to remain in training.

The drawbacks are equally obvious. Employers are likely to "cream" the disadvantaged workers, seeking those who best fill their needs. With or without subsidy, they will provide only the minimum necessary training for a given job, so that the participant will gain little which can be carried over if he is terminated from his JOBS position.

The JOBS program started off with much fanfare and apparently with a fair degree of success, though its achievements were usually exaggerated. Employers claimed reimbursement only for about one-fourth of the 230,000 hires in the first 18 months of the program. Many of these "freebies" were definitely among the hard-to-employ, though NAB thwarted Labor Department attempts to study their characteristics. This alleged success was used as justification for the rapid expansion of JOBS, though on a more modest scale than planned by the Johnson and Nixon administrations when enthusiasm for the program was rampant. Outlays were expected to rise from $43 million in fiscal 1969 to $128 million in the next year, and $200 million in fiscal 1971.

In 1970, expansion slowed to a halt as economic conditions became less favorable. The JOBS funds which had been earmarked in the anticipation of continued growth were re-allocated to other programs because of the meager participation of employers. This was not at all surprising. When employers are laying off workers, they are obviously not in the market for hiring more, especially

48

those who are less qualified than others seeking jobs. Of course, not all employers are affected by an overall economic setback, and those who continue to hire new employees may welcome subsidies for training the more attractive workers filling the ranks of the unemployed. However, in slack labor markets, both voluntary and subsidized participation cannot achieve the initial support given to the program, and the initial enthusiasm for JOBS dampened. Too often, however, economic decline is blamed for failures which have other causes. And though the administration was forced to cut back the program as a result of economic decline, the implicit assumption was that as inflationary policies are eased and unemployment rates fall, the JOBS approach can be effectively expanded, and that it will be as effective as the initial JOBS effort.

A closer look at the performance of the JOBS program even before the slump in business conditions not only deflates earlier appraisals, but indicates some of the constraints. Reported hiring figures were more than generous, especially in counting voluntary placements. As an example, one firm reported to have hired 300 "freebies" had only 2,000 employees, had experienced a strike during the period, and had certified only 100 of these workers as disadvantaged by sending in hire cards. Many more cases of this type have been experienced. But even where the hires were real, and "disadvantaged" persons were employed, they were often those who would have gotten the jobs in the absence of the program. Ford Motor Company hired approximately 3,000 disadvantaged workers between October 1967 and April 1968—mostly before the NAB efforts were initiated—and its efforts under JOBS served to create an altruistic aura around pragmatic practices. Other companies had been doing the same thing because of tight labor market conditions, and a very substantial share of those accredited to JOBS efforts were the same persons who would have been hired.

Little is known about the training offered under JOBS, but fragmentary evidence suggests that in many cases it is little more than what is normally offered. Most of the "freebies" received at most some orientation and job coaching, and even contract training was in many cases negligible. The large subsidies were apparently more for hiring than for training; for instance, $3,600 was given for training janitors in one case, $3,900 for laborers, and $3,400 for office boys. Though these are not typical, it is unlikely that training costs for the entry-level jobs filled by most hires amounted to the $3,000 average subsidy.

Whatever success the JOBS program may have had in the past, two major factors indicate constraints to expansion. Voluntary participation by employers has very definite limitations, and hires cannot be expanded simply by increasing appeals to corporate conscience. One of the important reasons why businesses participated in JOBS was the publicity value. As more firms hire disadvantaged workers and advertise their commitment, the value diminishes—as it would over time anyway. It is likely that this limit has already been reached and that the scale of voluntary efforts will never be greater than in late 1968 and early 1969. For instance, the National Alliance of Businessmen was once staffed by volunteers on loan from large corporations; now, probably a majority are government employees because volunteers cannot be found. The assistant vice-president on his way up may be glad to work in an expanding area where his firm is increasingly committed; but he is unlikely to want to take on long-run obligations and responsibilities outside his job.

If voluntary efforts will not expand, subsidies will clearly have to be increased to enlarge the scale of the program. The firms which can most effectively hire and train disadvantaged workers will be the first to participate, with low subsidy demands. To attract a firm with little use for such efforts, greater incentives will be needed. There is very definitely a saturation point, or a limit to the proportion of disadvantaged which any company can afford or is willing to employ, and it is likely that many firms have reached this limit.

As costs inevitably rise, or even if they remain at present levels, it is critical to ask whether these are justified. Is it worth $3,000 per year—and the turnover rate is so high that the subsidies can hardly be considered a one-shot proposition—to place a "disadvantaged" worker in a private and usually entry-level job? Perhaps, if there were careful policing to insure that those being hired would probably not have otherwise been employed, that training is intensive and provides a foundation for advancement, and that the seriously disadvantaged are served. But such safeguards are difficult to implement if the goal is also expansion. Increased private sector participation will probably be purchased at an impractically high price.

Even in the past, the subsidy may have been too large. One appraisal of the JOBS program funded by the Labor Department concluded that most of the contract jobs were low-skill and vulnerable to technological change, that the moderately disadvantaged workers who were hired could probably have found similar jobs on their own, and that they would benefit more if trained in more marketable skills. To the degree that this is the case, the expansion of the JOBS approach in even the most favorable of conditions is unwarranted unless changes are made to improve its impact on the disadvantaged worker.

Welfare vs. Workfare

The effort to reduce expanding relief rolls by training recipients for work dates from the early 1960s. The Community Work and Training Program of 1962 was the first, though half-hearted, attempt to implement the "rehabilitation not relief" philosophy, authorizing federal funds for the employment of male family heads receiving Aid to Families with Dependent Children. On a much larger scale, Title V of the Economic Opportunity Act initiated the Work Experience and Training Program, also for the training and employment of AFDC recipients, though other needy persons participated. The Work Incentive Program (WIN) was established by 1967 amendments to the Social Security Act, eventually replacing Title V, but restricted only to recipients of assistance. Under WIN, participants were allowed to keep $30 a month plus a third of their earnings against offsetting reductions in relief payments. The provision was intended as an incentive to seek employment and went hand in hand with training to increase employability.

51

The WIN program has received increasing emphasis under the Nixon Administration, and plans called for an enrollment of 125,000 by the end of fiscal 1970, making it the largest single manpower program administered by the Labor Department. More than this, the administration has proposed a new welfare measure, the Family Assistance Plan, which would extend and increase work incentives for all AFDC recipients as well as providing income subsidies for the working poor.

Given the eight years' experience with subsidized employment of relief recipients, the expansion of WIN and the new welfare proposals are supposedly grounded on sound evidence of success in training and placing welfare recipients and consequently in reducing welfare rolls. As the 1970 *Manpower Report* puts it, "the Work Incentive Program . . . has in its brief history provided a foundation for the much larger program of family assistance that would be authorized by the Administration's proposed Family Assistance Act."

This claim is not based on hard facts, which are in extremely short supply in this case. What is known about WIN provides a doubtful basis for its continuation at present levels, much less for large-scale welfare reforms (which may be needed and justified for other reasons). A total of 167,000 had enrolled in WIN through April 30, 1970. More than a third had dropped out, and of the 89,000 enrolled in the fall of 1970, nearly a third were in the intake, assessment, orientation, or holding stages, which chiefly involved waiting for placement. All tolled, only 25,000 had moved on to work, half of whom were supposedly enabled to move off welfare rolls. Those who found jobs were among the earliest participants and were definitely "creamed." They included a large percentage of employable fathers receiving AFDC-UP who could be put to work most easily and who would have most likely found jobs in the absence of WIN. What the long-range experience of these workers will be is not known, but it should not be a surprise to any observers that in slack labor markets severe difficulties are being experienced in finding jobs for current enrollees.

Experience with WIN's predecessors would suggest that its long-run impact might not be large. Though the Title V WE&T program provided public rather than private employment for the most part, its costs per enrollee, presumably for training as well as work-related expenses, were slightly higher than average under WIN; the differences between WE&T public employment and "holding in training" under WIN are not large. Follow-up studies of WE&T have indicated little evidence that participation in the program led to permanently increased earnings. The incentives provided in 1967 to seek employment might have increased the desire to work among recipients of public assistance, but there is no reason to presume that they would have done so more for trainees than for nontrainees who were equally eligible to benefit from the work incentives.

Based on this conspicuously unspectacular performance, the wisdom of expanding WIN is questionable, and the theoretical arguments for such a move are even more dubious. Certainly it is desirable to substitute self-support for relief, but the costs of training, providing work incentives and day care, and creating public employment or subsidizing employment where jobs are not available, may substantially exceed any savings in welfare payments. The Department of Health, Education, and Welfare estimates the costs of after-school and summer care for school-age children at $400 per year, and for full-day preschoolers at $1,600. The average AFDC family has three children. If a mother has one child under six, and one in school but still requiring attention, the annual cost will be $2,000 if other arrangements cannot be made. Training under WIN averages around $1,250 per slot, while its work incentives allow the recipient to retain $30 per month plus 30 percent of earnings. The income disregard provisions under the proposed Family Assistance Plan would be $60 plus 50 percent of the balance. If the family earned the $2,000 they currently average from AFDC, and probably only a third could earn this amount according to studies of recipients, welfare payments would be reduced by only $973 under WIN and $280 under FAP. Thus, for $2,000 in day-care subsidies and $1,250 in training, WIN would reduce welfare payments by $973 and FAP by $280. But despite the popular belief that jobs are available for anyone seeking employment, the low and declining placement rates under WIN would indicate that few employers are seeking workers from public assistance rolls. Proposals have been introduced to increase public employment or to subsidize private employers to absorb WIN trainees. The latter measure typically costs around $3,000 per slot, if JOBS experience is to be taken as a guide, and public employment would increase public outlays per person. To bring a family up to $3,000 earnings, $1,640 would be saved under WIN at a cost of more than $5,000. The argument that training is a one-shot proposition and that AFDC mothers will continue to work long after their children no longer need attention does not carry much weight when most studies reveal that: women work anyway when their children are old enough; AFDC would be cut off at any rate when the youngest child reached 18; the jobs for which they are trained are hardly lifetime positions; and future child-bearing is very likely to interrupt work experience.

This is not to deny that many may benefit from training and for them it will be a cost-effective expenditure. Certainly this would include male family heads receiving AFDC-UP, female heads with access to free or low-cost child care facilities, or those whose children have grown up. But WIN has not demonstrated the degree of success which would justify expansion even in serving such a select clientele, at least under present conditions.

Some would argue that substituting "workfare for welfare" is worth whatever price may be involved (though these are usually the same persons who believe that jobs are available for anyone who wants to work and that almost all welfare recipients can and should work). Few would deny that a working family head sets a better example than one who lives on the dole; it is probable that welfare begets welfare to some degree. However, the lack of education, adequate diet, and good housing have a demonstrated effect on the probability of dependency. The money used to create work, if a positive cost is involved, could be applied to other ends which might reduce future welfare rolls. Little is known about intergenerational effects of receiving welfare, or the impact of creating a working family head and putting the children in day care. Without evidence, those arguing for jobs at any cost cannot be proved wrong, and the price which is to be paid in substituting welfare for workfare must be resolved politically. The economist attempting to pass judgment on whether WIN should be reduced or expanded can only point to the facts that in slack labor markets there will be increasing difficulties and rising costs to place WIN recipients in jobs. The decision to expand WIN must be based on other grounds than the claim that it is a productive investment.

UPGRADING

A new thrust in the manpower effort is an emphasis on the quality as well as the quantity of employment opportunities. Dead-end jobs are not a long-run solution to the needs of disadvantaged workers, and optimally everyone should have the chance to move up with the acquisition of new skills and abilities. The idea of upgrading poorly paid workers has an intuitive and basic appeal.

Unfortunately, efforts to support upgrading have met with little success. The major program in this area has been New Careers, though its enrollment never passed 4,000. New Careers provides grants to local agencies covering the full wage of trainees for one year, and half for the next, as they are given training and work experience in subprofessional, human service jobs. The agencies are then expected to continue to hire and eventually to upgrade these workers. Their jobs are to be restructured and artificial credential barriers broken down, opening avenues to advancement. Though several projects have been notably successful, New Careers as a whole has not lived up to expectations. Most of the "subprofessional" jobs have been little more than the usual low-paying service employment, or else busy-work created to use allotted funds. Professionals have resisted efforts to break down credentials barriers and to restructure jobs, many positions have been terminated once subsidies stopped, and the turnover rate

ESTABLISHING PRIORITIES

among New Careers trainees has been high for a program promising substantial long-run benefits.

While few would be so bold to suggest that New Careers has been a success, even fewer challenge the idea that upgrading is necessary and possible for disadvantaged workers. In this case, the failure of the program has not challenged the underlying approach, but has been blamed on poor implementation. In fact, a much-expanded Public Service Careers (PSC) program was announced in early 1970. It would include New Careers projects and would also provide funds for the extra training and education needed to employ and upgrade disadvantaged workers in state and local government, especially under grant-in-aid programs, as well as in the federal civil service. It is projected that in fiscal 1971 PSC will reach an enrollment of 32,000, a vast increase over New Careers levels.

Upgrading is also to be given increased priority under JOBS. Subsidies are now offered for special training programs to advance already hired workers trapped in dead-end jobs, and some assistance is available for upgrading workers of higher quality where there are severe skill shortages. There has been little response yet to these incentives, but the hope is that JOBS hires will eventually gain more meaningful employment, with or without extra subsidies.

As long as these efforts are pursued on an experimental basis, with careful examination and analysis of cost and benefits, and with a limited commitment of resources, the projects are worth serious study for the lessons that may be gleaned from them. In framing this experiment, however, several factors should be kept in mind.

A very real and present danger is the "numbers game," which can be played even more loosely in upgrading than in programs offering training for entry-level jobs. Private employers have traditionally offered training and education for employees, and subsidies to employers might be simply a transfer of the burden to the government, without markedly increasing the quality or distribution of training.

56

Moreover, it is difficult to insure that upgrading efforts serve their purpose. Upgrading efforts are addressed to a much larger universe of need than earlier attempts to find jobs for those with limited employability. Unemployed, disadvantaged workers would be candidates for newly created entry-level positions with upgrading potential, but, in addition, the millions of persons employed in dead-end jobs could not be denied the same opportunities as the present clients of the manpower programs. There are millions of low-level jobs in this country with little upgrading potential, offering low wages and unattractive working conditions. Only a very small proportion of these jobs can be restructured and only a limited number of workers can be helped. Despite the wish that everyone move up, there must be a fairly large number of Indians for every chief, and though opportunities can and should be opened so that everyone has an equal chance to don the headdress, the structure of jobs cannot be drastically changed. At best, only a small portion of the universe of need can benefit from upgrading efforts.

Whether in public or private employment, "creaming" will necessarily be carefully practiced, as candidates for upgrading will have to be screened more closely than those for entry-level jobs. One likely result is that women will benefit more from upgrading than men, as has occurred under New Careers, since past discrimination and child care responsibilities have left a larger number of better educated women who qualify for public service jobs. These likely developments are welcomed, but they suggest a direction contrary to prevailing rhetoric which extols upgrading priorities for male heads of families.

A related policy decision is whether upgrading will emphasize one-step improvements for a large number of persons, or career opportunities for a necessarily smaller number. The two are often confused, and this can lead to misconceptions about cost and the number who will be helped.

Whatever the scale of upgrading efforts, if these are selectively applied to disadvantaged and usually black workers, animosities will be aroused among those not receiving help. It is necessary to give minority group members special attention in order to equalize opportunities, but to concentrate preferential treatment on a minority group, especially in opening up better positions, is to invite opposition to manpower programs. Many already claim that the manpower programs must give increased attention to solving the problems of blue-collar workers—the presumably alienated middle Americans.

The caveats listed here strongly suggest that upgrading efforts must be expanded cautiously. These efforts are definitely not a substitute for the present manpower programs. As long as manpower resources are limited, emphasis should probably be given to helping those with the most severe problems. While there are still many workers who cannot find full-time jobs, and while there are proven methods of assisting these workers, it would seem unwise to shift resources to untested methods of helping those who are better off, even if their problems are still severe.

The Choices To Be Made

The emphasis by the Nixon administration on inducing private employer participation, "workfare instead of welfare," and upgrading, is not grounded in past experimentation. Claims to the contrary may be considered mostly political rhetoric. What is not well understood is the role which experimentation can and should play in determining priorities, as well as the inherent limitations of this role.

Priorities involve choices between alternative claimants for scarce resources. There are a wide range of people who could use help, of needs which they have, and of approaches to meeting these needs. The allocation of funds requires choices among persons, needs, and approaches and should be based on substantive information. To determine the universe of need, separate clienteles must be identified, the seriousness of their problems examined, and the likelihood and cost of solving them determined. The efficacy of different approaches must be considered, including both the costs they entail and the benefits they are likely to produce.

Even the best available information is inadequate for policy determination unless it is combined with normative concepts of trade-offs and values. For instance, one program might serve youths by providing basic education, while another gives them placement services. The choice between them is fairly clearcut if it can be determined which has the most effect on employability per dollar of expenditures—that is, as long as no positive weight is given to education or to work *per se.* Choosing between younger and older participants for the above programs complicates matters even more and involves decisions about the relative importance of each group, the effectiveness of different programs in serving each group, the consequences of increasing resources for one group at the expense of another, and many other factors.

If all of these are given explicit consideration, the process of determining priorities becomes almost imponderable. Decisions are not reached in this way. Principles and values are rarely articulated, and the trade-offs are usually not pinned down. Vague concepts are combined with available information to come out with what seems to be the "best" choice. The role of social experimentation is to provide a substantive basis for decisions so that, when feasible, normative considerations can be separated from substantive ones.

There are dangers, however, in insisting upon too much rationality in determining priorities. Large-scale changes are probably discouraged by such an approach. Opponents of change can always demand more experimentation and a more "measured" pace of expansion. Since flaws can usually be spotted in any plan, the demand for more data and evaluations or criticism of existing programs can be a cover for differing principles and values than those supporting evolving priorities. The "war on poverty" might still be limited to a few isolated projects if original plans had been followed. The rhetoric of total war gave impetus to expanded funding (albeit inadequate to the rhetoric).

Thus, despite the evidence and logical arguments against expansion of private sector programs, remedial services and work incentives for welfare recipients, and upgrading efforts, these efforts may still be warranted. Their basic concepts may be given an especially high priority, demanding that the means to these ends be worked out even though there are obstacles. Private sector participation may be considered vital so that those provided with remedial services can be placed in private rather than public sector employment. Checking the growth of welfare rolls, especially where employable family heads are concerned, may be a critical goal. Certainly providing better jobs for those in dead-end employment is a worthy pursuit which has received little attention in the past. If these goals are given high priority, the shortcomings of existing efforts in these directions may be overlooked.

Issues of priority are never clearcut. The balance between reasoned consideration of available evidence and energetic implementation of differing principles is difficult to achieve and even more difficult to analyze in the abstract. In regard to the three programs discussed in this section, it is a judgment that the proper balance was not achieved and that existing data and evaluations were not given enough weight. Others, especially those involved in the decisions, may have different criteria and may feel that available evidence was given due consideration. Certainly, however, these decisions should be continuously re-examined as more information becomes available, and changes should be made accordingly.

6
Improving Administration

THE RHETORIC: Improved planning, coordination, and administration will substantially increase the effectiveness of the manpower programs.

THE REALITY: Administrative changes are needed, but they are likely to effect only marginal improvements in the manpower programs.

It is self-evident that the manpower programs will have a greater impact if they are better planned, better coordinated, and better administered. It is also obvious that there is room for improvement in all these areas. Manpower planning has been minimal because of the hasty development and implementation of the programs. Coordination has been noticeably lacking as a variety of agencies at all levels of government have tried to establish claims on expanding manpower resources. Administration has suffered from the frequent changes in design and emphasis, and from shortages of qualified personnel.

The obvious need for improvement in these areas has led to repeated reorganizational efforts in the past: new comprehensive reorganizations have been proposed at the same time. These, it is claimed, will markedly improve the effectiveness of the manpower programs. However, a careful examination of previous experience suggests that there are formidable obstacles and that administrative reforms will have a limited impact. In advocating improvements, it is often necessary to make inflated promises in order to overcome opposition; and when the improvements do not materialize, the effectiveness of the changes is disparaged. The setbacks suffered by the manpower programs because of this process are therefore no argument against further attempts to improve efficiency of operations and overhauling of delivery systems, but the limitations of administrative changes must be understood.

EVOLVING PROBLEMS

Since the manpower programs were breaking new ground, and since they were changed and expanded at a rapid pace, there was little basis or time for planning. The programs were fleshed out as quickly as possible, staffs were assembled, and adjustments were made as real or imaginary crises arose. Without some evidence of program performance, which could only come with time, this was the only possible course of action. States and localities had little control over the use of manpower monies, while the federal government relied on fixed formulas or project-by-project determinations to make allocations. Funds remained scarce relative to needs, and manpower planning was given a low priority in the early years of the decade since there were ample claimants for all available resources and criteria were lacking for establishing priorities among efforts. By the time there was a firmer basis for making decisions, and a greater need with states and localities having more control, vested interests had been established, competing for a larger piece of the action.

Since various levels of government and local sponsoring groups had varied responsibilities and controls under the different programs there was no basis for comprehensive planning. Thus planning could be little more than a nominal gesture, and the recommendations emanating from planning were necessarily a compromise between competing interests. Behind the scenes was a bureaucratic struggle for territorial rights. At the national level, the Office of Economic Opportunity, the Department of Health, Education, and Welfare, and the Department of Labor vied with one another for control over the programs. The scattering of authority among these different agencies was a necessary compromise to get the manpower effort underway and some less than friendly bedpartners were created. MDTA institutional training was to be provided by vocational educators with the Department of Labor as a senior partner, while OJT was to be administered by the Department of Labor alone. The operation of the Job Corps conservation centers was delegated to the Departments of Agriculture and the Interior and a few states, while the urban centers and the programs as a whole were to be run by OEO. The Vocational Rehabilitation program of HEW was extended to those with "socioeconomic" as well as physical difficulties; this placed it in potential competition with the newer programs which served the same clientele, although, unlike the vocational educators, the officials of Vocational Rehabilitation avoided any embroilment. In-school NYC projects were developed by the educational establishment, while the out-of-school and summer programs were to be operated by the Labor Department with the doubtful benefit of OEO kibitzing. A now defunct work experience program for welfare recipients was delegated to HEW, which attempted to run the program alone with minimum involvement of the Employment Service.

Working relationships developed, but continuing conflicts at the national level exacerbated the even more difficult problems at the state and local level. OEO's administration of manpower programs drew particular criticism from the established agencies because of its advocacy of community control, and gradually its authority diminished, with the Department of Labor gaining control over all but two small OEO programs as the enabling legislation underwent repeated amendments.

Despite this consolidation of authority, other departments, especially HEW, continued to vie for control and for funds. There was also a fair degree of jockeying between agencies within the Labor Department. For instance, until the opposition of labor unions and employment service lobbies was overcome in 1969, three separate bureaus shared responsibility for various manpower programs and often operated at cross purposes. Each defended its prerogatives as if it were an independent body, even though all three were in the Labor Department.

At the local level, the lack of coordination occasionally bordered on chaos. Some funds were allocated directly to the states on the basis of fixed formulas spelled out by Congress. Other funds were granted to governmental or private agencies on a project-by-project basis. Cities and sponsors mastering the art of grantsmanship received disproportionate amounts of funds. The attempted justification—that duplication generated competition (which was supposed to improve efficiency)—was the last refuge of apologists who could not find a better rationalization for a difficult situation. Duplication, competition, and waste were often present, probably to a greater degree than in other, more established federal efforts. For instance, outreach and adult basic education were available under 11 different programs, prevocational and skill training from 10, OJT from five. The eligibility rules, allocation formulas, and application procedures varied under each, so that it was extremely difficult to piece them together into a comprehensive program.

These problems were complicated by the struggles for power, arraying state governments against local agencies, vocational educators against OJT sponsors, and community groups against city hall. Under the OEO programs, the general approach was to contract directly with these community groups on the assumption that these would better reflect the needs of OEO clients and would provide some needed competition to established governmental agencies. Public employment offices were prime targets since many community action agency leaders charged that the employment service had neglected the disadvantaged. Not surprisingly, these agencies and the city halls shared little of the enthusiasm for community control.

ADMINISTRATIVE REFORM: THE ONE-STOP CONCEPT

While authority over the manpower programs was gradually being consolidated at the national level within the Departments of Labor and HEW, several attempts were made to improve planning, coordination, and administration locally. In early 1967, the Concentrated Employment Program (CEP) was launched with the dual intent of concentrating limited funds on a few target areas and creating a single agency to tie together the separate programs operating in a locality. The local CEP was intended to be a one-stop center, which could provide some services itself, purchase others, or refer the applicant to other agencies—thus insuring that each person would receive the package of services he needed.

CEP was unable to meet these objectives. At the outset, a jurisdictional conflict erupted between local OEO-funded agencies and the United States Employment Service (since changed to United States Training and Employment Service). While community action agencies were to be the program sponsors in each area, the Employment Service was to be the "presumptive provider of manpower services." This Solomon-like division of authority led to immediate conflict between the rival agencies, heated by the difficulties of many community action agencies to recruit experienced and competent personnel to administer and staff the CEPs. Furthermore, MDT institutional training, and later the JOBS program, remained outside CEP control, undercutting its role as a one-stop, comprehensive service agency. Funds for staffing and for direct assistance were meager, and the expansion in coverage from the original 22 to 82 areas meant that resources were spread thinly, precluding concentrated impact. As a result of all this, the CEP program has been a failure in most areas, unable to deliver jobs or training slots. Instead of coordinating the existing programs, it has simply complicated the situation by adding another layer of administration.

65

COORDINATION AND REGIONALIZATION

While the CEP approach aimed at coordinating manpower programs locally, the Cooperative Area Manpower Planning System (CAMPS) was initiated to increase state planning and coordination, largely through the governor's office, which usually delegated the responsibility to the state employment services. State committees were to consolidate area plans into a comprehensive scheme. Some anticipated that the state would become the funnel for federal funds so that local governments and sponsors would apply directly to it rather than to a variety of sources. At the least it was expected that CAMPS would bring together and plug holes in disparate efforts.

This was not the way it turned out. Most of the state plans were little more than the consolidation of the separate local and participating state agency reports. A few states took an active role, creating "super" manpower agencies and increasing their control over the distribution of funds, but for the most part the plans were useless. The feds were not anxious to release their purse strings and few funds were administered through CAMPS, which consequently had little power to change priorities or to reallocate resources. In all but a few states, CAMPS had no clout and the manpower "plans" they spun were of doubtful value—ignored by those concerned with getting money and operating programs.

Another attempt at improving coordination among the programs came in 1968 when the Labor Department announced the regionalization of its authority to eight (later changed to 10) regional manpower offices. These were expected to play an important role in decentralization, planning, and coordination, since the Labor Department's programs accounted for about two-thirds of all manpower funds. Such has not been the case. The regional manpower administrators and their staffs are federal officials with no more roots in local or state developments than their counterparts in Washington, and the major contribution of the regional offices is that they saved some local sponsors transportation expenses; instead of traveling to Washington they now go hat in hand to the regional offices. The new system has resulted in little change from the former centralized administrative structure, but it lends itself to impressive rhetoric that governmental functions are being decentralized and that the government is being brought to the people.

THE PITFALLS OF PLANNING, COORDINATION, AND SIMPLIFICATION

The continued changes in the structure of programs and in their level of funding have remained a constant obstacle to manpower planning. With appropriations on a year-to-year basis and no assurance that substantive provisions will remain unchanged, planning can consist of little more than the compilation of project needs and proposals. Since needs are so great in any area relative to available assistance, it does not matter much what set of services is emphasized. More important is that money is channeled to successful projects, which requires flexibility in allocating funds and administrative fortitude more than careful planning.

Even if these obstacles were eliminated, there are some inherent shortcomings to planning; and despite the lip-service and resources devoted to it, manpower planning may not be especially effective. Essentially, its major function is to allocate available resources among competing ends. Without the ability to enforce such allocations, planning becomes pointless, as it has for the most part under CAMPS. If planning is combined with authority, the planning agency becomes necessarily an operating agency and, of course, the target of those who are shortchanged by its allocations. When planning and administrative authority are combined, advocacy often takes the place of objective analysis.

Coordination of separate efforts and cooperation among competing agencies are perhaps even rarer than successful planning. Voluntary and *ad hoc* agreements can sometimes be reached between congenial administrators, resulting in lasting operational relationships, but this is the exception rather than the rule. Whether at the national, state, or local level, bureaucrats tend to identify with their own programs and view any loss in authority as a personal loss. At the local level, the power base of many groups lies in their authority over some manpower service and its funding; its loss would undermine the agency itself. For instance, any transfer of authority from the community action agencies to employment service offices or the mayors' offices could wipe out many of these groups, which would surely be viewed as an act of aggrandizement by the affected establishment. While administrators and community leaders may be amenable to "cooperation" in the abstract, their assumption is that "others will coo while we operate." This is hardly the foundation for true coordination.

Another lesson from past experience is that real-life programs are not always amenable to organization-chart simplifications. What appear to be administrative improvements may in fact confuse rather than simplify, upsetting working relationships, forcing changes or shifts in personnel and in jurisdictional boundaries, and often adding another administrative layer to those already in existence. Conditions vary so much from area to area, especially the capacities of local and state agencies to administer manpower programs, that any single organizational arrangement is a Procrustean bed. The failures of CEP and of CAMPS to provide a comprehensive administrative framework for the manpower programs—failures that wasted resources and energies which could have been used more productively—indicate the dangers of any superficial though "neat" exercises in administrative simplification.

COMPREHENSIVE ADMINISTRATIVE REFORMS

The formidable obstacles to administrative change have not discouraged proposals for comprehensive reforms. These proposals have essentially two thrusts: first, they would consolidate the legislative authorization of categorical programs, revising eligibility requirements, benefits, and the services offered so that they would be mutually compatible; and second, they would decentralize this consolidated authority to the state and local levels.

Consolidation would sidestep the problems of coordination. With single funding and compatible programs, the mix at the local and state levels could be more easily adjusted to meet needs and capabilities. Hopefully, this would result in a situation where each area would be able to provide any of the whole range of manpower services to participants depending on their needs. Toward this end, the proposals would consolidate the programs administered by the Labor Department, though other important manpower programs, such as Vocational Education and Rehabilitation, would remain independent because of the power of their lobbies to resist any transfer of control.

The consolidation and decentralization of authority are intended to provide better adaptation to local conditions and political accountability for the distribution of funds. One proposal would allocate 75 percent of funds to states on the basis of need, with 25 percent retained for national and experimental projects, for research and for incentive grants to states and localities. Another would also allocate funds to the states, dependent on the development of a long-term comprehensive plan, but with guaranteed "pass through" of funds to designated sponsors (usually local governments) in metropolitan areas. A third approach would consolidate authority within the Labor Department, allowing it to contract directly with state and local governments or private organizations; a fourth would allow every city or county with a population of over 75,000 or 100,000 to apply directly to the Labor Department for a block grant.

These differences are significant. They involve complex issues and manifest differing conceptions of the proper role of federal, state and local governments, not to mention the community groups operating outside the governmental structure. If funds are distributed from Washington, coordination, planning, and adaptation to local conditions will presumably suffer. Time and time again, those in the field trying to solve local problems have charged that inflexibility at the federal level has made it extremely difficult to put together the optimal package of services. Federal officials simply cannot know the capabilities and needs of every locality. On the other hand, authority has been centralized and categorized because of (among other things) a shortage of qualified administrators and planners. Though more and more people have become experienced in the manpower field, shortages are still severe and national programs are still the best way of utilizing limited expertise.

If funds are given directly to states, most of which have not developed a capability to plan, design, and administer manpower programs, all services may suffer and urban areas may be neglected. Large city halls are especially sensitive about any increase in the state role because they feel that most of the problems are concentrated in urban areas, that a political imbalance still exists which would shortchange funds for the cities, and that many metropolitan areas are better qualified and experienced to administer the manpower programs than their state governments. On the other hand, if the programs are operated autonomously by local governments, community groups which now deliver manpower services and are often a useful countervailing force against city halls, will wither away. The proper balance between community and local government control is an especially touchy subject. Antipoverty, manpower, and Model Cities measures have taken different approaches to the problem with different degrees of success. Perhaps an even greater problem from the standpoint of evaluating social experimentation is that as control is decentralized, and as block grants are increasingly used, it will become even more difficult to measure the aggregate impact of federal monies, to test alternate approaches, or to find out whether desired ends are being served. It is no accident that the best statistics to date are available for the federally operated Job Corps program, while the worst are those of decentralized efforts, such as the Vocational Education and community action programs.

Diverse cures have been proposed to achieve the best of all possible worlds. The nostrums include complex incentive set-asides, categorical programs, guaranteed pass-throughs, and direct federal contracts with community groups; but these end up being little different than the system which already exists and sometimes even more complex or requiring, at least, adjustments to new rules of the game. If a compromise is to be reached, all of the agencies, levels of government, and community groups will want and will probably get their present share of manpower activity.

Not only will each operating agency defend its "rice bowl," but it is in these agencies that the needed expertise is concentrated. For the present, the programs will have to operate almost solely through existing channels using existing methods, until changes can be rationally engineered on the basis of careful decisions. Proposed administrative changes will probably have little immediate effect despite the fears and hopes of opposing groups that they will drastically upset the *status quo*.

The impact is likely to be manifested in the longer run. States and localities will be given a single source of funding rather than having to apply for separate programs with differing provisions. As they develop expertise, and as manpower funds are expanded, they can begin to construct a mix of programs most suited to their needs. But to expect immediate improvement is naive. The competition among agencies will persist, even if it is shifted from the federal to the state and local level. Planning will still involve the resolution of competing demands for limited funds, and, as such, it will move into the electoral arena as authority is transferred to agencies with political accountability. The administration of the programs will still be limited by the scarcity of skilled manpower at all levels of government. In other words, improved planning, coordination, and administration can be gradually achieved and will increase the effectiveness of the manpower programs, but only over time.

7

Adapting to Economic Change

THE RHETORIC: Manpower programs can be adapted to changing economic conditions, and their effectiveness will not suffer.

THE REALITY: The effectiveness of the separate programs in slack conditions is not known, but major adjustments may be needed.

The five years between 1964 and 1969, when the manpower programs experienced their fastest expansion, were ones of steady growth and tight labor markets. Economic conditions later changed for the worse, and this may have a pervasive effect upon their performance. Unfortunately, recognition and reaction were slow. Legislators, administrators, and most manpower "experts" continued to carry on business as usual. There were proposals for increased manpower budgets and expanding public employment programs, but these were mostly reflex actions based on little thought. Because most manpower funds are appropriated for categorical programs, little can be done by administrative action; and Congressional delay in reacting to slack labor market conditions is based on the as yet unsubstantiated hope that manpower programs will adapt to change, or that comprehensive redirections are not needed, may prove to be costly.

THE CHANGING SCENARIO

With the rather abrupt decline in economic conditions in late 1969 and early 1970, unemployment rates rose from their 1969 average of 3.5 percent to 5.5 percent and higher during the following year. Even if unemployment declines with recovery and levels off at between 4.0 and 4.5 percent, it will take some time until these conditions prevail.

The precipitous rise in unemployment during 1970 meant that about 1.5 million more people were looking for work at any one time and that over the year several million experienced prolonged unemployment. Hundreds of thousands of discouraged workers left the labor market because of gloomy employment prospects. Though all occupational groups were affected, unemployment was concentrated among blue-collar workers and those at the end of the labor queue who suffer the most serious disadvantages in competing for existing jobs.

With rising unemployment, not only do increasing numbers of persons need manpower services, but there is also a change in the nature of the clients and the economic environment in which the manpower programs must function. Jobs are no longer plentiful, placements are not easy, more competent workers are now competing with the disadvantaged for available jobs, and businessmen are less willing to participate in manpower programs. The programs designed to aid the poor and unskilled in tight labor markets quite obviously must be adjusted to these changing circumstances.

MANPOWER PROGRAMS FOR ALL SEASONS

The challenge to manpower policy planners and administrators is to adapt programs to serve these new clients without ignoring the interests of their old clientele. The task is difficult not only because of budgetary constraints but also because manpower administrators have little experience in operating manpower programs in a labor market with rising unemployment. Several steps, however, can be suggested that would make economic sense.

Manpower programs oriented towards the private sector are likely to be more effective in tight labor market conditions than when slack occurs. Subsidies to hire and train disadvantaged workers, to induce business to locate in depressed areas, or to eliminate discrimination will have their greatest impact when qualified workers are not readily available, when firms are expanding and opening new plants, and when the supply of "preferred" workers has dried up. Conversely, when firms are forced to lay off employees because of declining demand, when they have excess capacity and are trying to eliminate all but their most efficient plants, and when fears of unemployment lead to employee antipathy toward newly hired disadvantaged workers, OJT or locational subsidies will be less effective. This has clearly been the experience under the JOBS programs, where terminations increased and hires decreased markedly in the economic decline at the end of 1969 and the beginning of 1970; in fact, funds originally earmarked for JOBS had to be reallocated to other manpower programs. The enrollment level rose slightly in late 1970 as employers found subsidies more attractive in a slack economy, but a significant expansion could not be achieved.

Public-sector training is virtually imperative in slack times, if for no other reason than to fill the gap left by declining private-sector participation (assuming that the level of funds allocated to manpower programs is maintained). Institutional training provides at least income maintenance and occasionally useful preparation for work along with basic education. In loose labor markets, the opportunities of potential enrollees to opt for jobs instead of training are reduced, and employers are less likely to pressure training institutions to speed the delivery of trainees. Under these circumstances, more persons are likely to participate in and complete a course of training under the manpower programs. Because placements and employment rates are closely correlated with duration of stay, institutional programs should become more effective.

It is also likely that manpower programs will serve a different clientele when unemployment is high than they did when jobs were plentiful. Increasingly during the 1960s, the more seriously disadvantaged workers were helped—in large part a result of expanding employment opportunities generally. The queue of job seekers moved forward rapidly and the disadvantaged, who were next in line for employment, were most in need of manpower services. But that manpower programs then emphasized the needs of the unskilled, poorly educated, and members of minority groups subject to discrimination does not mean that they will continue to do so. Under all the programs there has usually been a tendency to "cream" from the available and intended clientele those most likely to benefit from assistance. If demand slackens, it is safe to say that more advantaged workers will seek out and be selected for manpower programs; workers with more severe problems will receive less attention. For instance, in the JOBS program, as unemployment increased in 1970, the average family income of participants under contract increased steadily, indicating the selection of a less disadvantaged group. No doubt this is happening under other manpower programs, although data are not yet available to substantiate this change.

A fairly certain development is that disadvantaged workers will find it more and more difficult to secure employment in the private sector, and that they will likely fall into dependency. Because there are many useful jobs which need to be done in the public sector, many of which can be filled by those with low skills, public job creation gained support as an alternative to the expansion of relief rolls. The Senate approved a bill (S. 3867) which earmarked one-third of manpower funds for public employment projects, and the House favored a bill with more modest provisions for public employment (H. R. 19159). President Nixon vetoed the compromise version of these two bills, partly because he opposed expanded federal support of public employment.

Labor market services should also be adjusted to changing economic conditions. When jobs are plentiful, the public employment agencies function as labor exchanges; but they can also reach out to disadvantaged persons, providing them with needed counseling and help, inducing them to seek and find jobs. When unemployment is high, however, fewer firms turn to the public employment service offices, and those that do can choose among recently employed and less disadvantaged workers. If the needs of the disadvantaged are not to be ignored, this is exactly the time when job development and placement efforts should be intensified—even though they will be less successful in terms of placements. While the recently unemployed should be aided in their quest for work, the hard core must not be ignored; and if they cannot find private jobs, public employment or other manpower programs should be made available. Unfortunately, many employment service offices become bogged down administering an increasing unemployment insurance caseload during slack times, and thus play only a passive role as a labor exchange for the declining number of job offers. Some improvements have been made along these lines, with the physical separation of unemployment insurance and employment service offices in the major SMSAs and the hiring of part-time claims takers when needed; but employment services still suffer in slack times.

Taken together, these adjustments would suggest a strategy which runs as follows: when unemployment rises, manpower expenditures should be shifted into the areas of public employment and training because private employers will be less willing to hire and train disadvantaged workers, and because many previously hired will be laid off as a result of slackening demand. Institutional training and public employment must be expanded to assist such workers. Since enrollees are likely to stay longer in institutional programs, these can concentrate on basic education and the more serious problems of marginal workers. Adequate income support must also be provided. Private firms might be induced to perform a holding action by changing the focus of private-sector incentive programs from increasing the number of hires or relocating firms to reducing the number of workers who are dismissed or the number of depressed area plants which must be closed. The employment service must likewise increase job development and placement efforts for those recently unemployed, directing them to available manpower programs. Outreach efforts must necessarily be diminished, with a holding action again stressed.

Manpower programs were shifted, albeit too slowly, along these lines. While most experts would agree that such a strategy would maximize the impact of manpower programs in slack times, one must emphasize the uncertainty underlying these prescriptions. The simple fact is that we do not know how effective manpower programs can be at higher rates of unemployment. In all likelihood some will be better than others, but we cannot expect that overall they will have as favorable an impact in slack times—even though the need for them is more pressing.

Underlying the suggested strategy is the assumption that the shifts in program emphasis can be achieved efficiently and with little loss of time. Past performance in the administration of manpower programs does not necessarily support this assumption. In the present case, administration spokesmen were entirely too slow in acknowledging the economic downturn when it occurred; and needed adjustments in manpower programs were delayed.

The Potential of Public Employment

At the center of the proposed shifts of manpower efforts is greater emphasis upon public employment. The normal reaction is to launch and expand job creation when unemployment rises, and this was the case during the 1970 decline.

Expansion of public employment is probably a wise strategy, but it is not above question. Certainly the evidence of its effectiveness is mixed, and it has hardly been subjected to careful analysis. In tight labor markets, there is little interest in public employment programs, while during economic downturns arguments are hastily mounted to get programs underway. Many misconceptions prevail, and these should be cleared up before any large-scale commitments are made.

Public job creation to absorb the unemployed reached its peak during the New Deal. The Public Works Administration, the Works

Progress Administration, and the Civilian Conservation Corps provided income and work for millions of people. Despite the image of the leaf-raking WPA worker which still persists, many workers must have done more than a fair day's labor: the thousands of buildings and hundreds of thousands of highway miles attest to the useful work performed by the New Deal public employment agencies. If a cost-benefit ratio could be applied to these programs, there is little doubt that they would prove extremely worthwhile.

More recent experience with public employment programs has been less favorable. The Work Experience and Training Program initiated under the 1964 "war on poverty" was addressed to a potential clientele numbering more than 2 million, and it was hoped that eventually the program could reach the majority of these people. By 1968 the program had been dropped, with general agreement that it fell far short of intended goals. Out-of-school NYC, another antipoverty effort, started out with high hopes and reached a point where 189,000 slots were planned in fiscal 1966. Here, too, performance was judged to be deficient, and the program was later cut back to some 32,000 slots. Only Operation Mainstream, a public works program serving mostly older workers in rural areas, has been favorably received, though it has remained a very modest effort.

Public employment programs have been de-emphasized the last few years because of the increasing availability of jobs in the private sector, but also because the programs have shared certain shortcomings. First, they were rapidly expanded and then contracted, so that the enrollees' work could not be well planned. While it is difficult to measure the value of work done, available evidence indicates that it was slight. Participants in the programs did not seem to benefit apart from the income they received. The limited dosages of education and counseling consumed a fair amount of time and money, but there is no persuasive evidence that the services improved the enrollees' later work experience. The jobs which were created lacked attraction and carried little prestige, and in many areas there were difficulties in filling available slots. If the analysis of some labor market economists is correct, many similarly unattractive jobs in the private sector also remained unfilled, and in such areas it was simply wasteful to create new jobs in the public sector. For the most part, public employment projects were merely stopgap measures, with few permanently beneficial effects and even questionable impact at the time. Perhaps such jobs were preferable to income transfers, but they were hardly equal to manpower services with a long-run payoff.

Operation Mainstream, which provides public employment in rural conservation work, is a notable exception. The clientele is older, so that basic education and vocational training are not important components. Enrollees' time is productively utilized because very little is spent on training. Since participants would probably be otherwise unemployed, and many of their families on assistance, any positive contribution they can make is all to the good. Clearly the ingredients to success in Operation Mainstream could be duplicated in more rural areas where job deficits exist, but only for a similar clientele.

From this mixed experience, it is difficult to arrive at a clear judgment on the effectiveness of public employment programs. It should be obvious, however, that the term covers many different types of activities, ranging from simple conservation work under Operation Mainstream to paraprofessional positions under New Careers; it can serve a range of clienteles, from elderly workers desiring an income supplement to youths who need preparation for future labor force participation; it can be planned as a temporary measure to cushion the effects of a short-term slump or a long-run measure to combat secular changes in the economic structure.

Unfortunately, these distinctions are too often ignored. Arguments for increased public employment, bolstered by public concern over rising unemployment rates, tend to follow rather simplistic lines. Public employment is urged by those who believe that "structural unemployment" has increased markedly, as more and more workers become obsolete because of technological change. While unemployment rates had fallen prior to the 1970 recession among the disadvantaged, and income has increased in recent years, much of this has been due—they argue—to an arbitrary statistical decision not to count enrollees in manpower programs as unemployed or to exclude them from labor force statistics and to the induction into the armed forces of an additional 800,000 men, many of whom would have been unemployed or else would have filled jobs opened to disadvantaged workers. With increasing or higher unemployment rates, many of these more disadvantaged workers are unable to find private sector jobs. The proper course of action, according to the structuralists, is to generate public employment for those who cannot find jobs in the open market.

Supporters are also found among those who see the needs for large numbers of less skilled workers in the rapidly expanding public service areas, such as health, education, sanitation, welfare work, and conservation. Though estimates of job vacancies in public employment are suspect and may frequently be blown up to support claims of unmet needs, they have ranged from more than 5 million for the nation in 1966, assuming costless labor, to 300,-000 in 130 large cities in 1968, based on surveys of mayors' estimates. Whatever the precise number, it is apparent that hundreds of thousands of persons could be absorbed in highly productive full-time public employment.

The most common mistake is to equate estimated job vacancies with actual openings. Various pressing needs always compete for available resources, and in allocating additional funds, the authorities may opt for constructing new facilities rather than hiring new workers. Even if it is decided to hire additional workers, it would be incorrect to assume that this need can be filled by those who are unemployed, or that supply can be efficiently matched with demand through a subsidized public employment program. Real life is much more complex. For instance, Mayor Carl Stokes of Cleveland estimated in the summer of 1970 that only 2,900 of the 6,900 additional positions needed by his city could be filled, with training, by disadvantaged unemployed persons; 4,000 of the jobs would require more highly skilled workers not found among the clientele of the manpower programs. Certainly Mayor Stokes would not deliberately underestimate the potential utilization of disadvantaged workers. Given a choice, most cities would probably fill their skill needs first; and at least they would require many additional qualified or credentialed employees before they could effectively use the unskilled and deficiently educated, who would require training before they could become fully productive. Of course, if money were provided with strings attached, any group could be put to work as long as no questions were raised about the value of the work or the productivity of the labor hired.

Unskilled manpower can be utilized in rural conservation work, which remains labor-intensive despite the use of machines to do much of the work which was performed manually in the New Deal days. The problem is that the disadvantaged in urban areas have never expressed great enthusiasm for the idea of moving to rural areas in order to accept minimum wage jobs. Unless unemployment rates are extremely high, as they are for youths in the summer, it is unlikely that the public needs for workers in rural areas will be met from the pool of unemployed in the cities.

Finally, most of the needs, especially in urban areas, are for full-time, long-term workers. But economic slumps since World War II have lasted on the average less than a year. While one might think offhand that numerous tasks could be performed by an enlarged public work force during periods of temporarily high unemployment, the experience of summer NYC suggests the acute difficulties of putting enrollees to work, even at present operating levels. Especially in large cities, there may not be a very large demand for temporary unskilled employees. It is only a hope that more effective organizational efforts will expand the demand for unskilled personnel who would fill temporary vacancies and perhaps eventually fill the jobs on a permanent basis.

It should thus be clear that the case for or against public employment as a counter-cyclical measure is not conclusive. We do not know whether a large-scale effort can be effectively implemented in a short time, putting a large number of disadvantaged persons to productive work, or whether this is an attractive alternative to monetary and fiscal measures increasing aggregate demand. Lacking proof, public employment efforts must themselves be viewed as experiments and should not be promoted as proven solutions to evolving economic problems.

That measurement and evaluation of public employment efforts in the past does not supply straightforward answers about their likely impact under 1970s conditions is understandable. These conditions differ significantly and the components of proposed programs change. Yet past experiences should not be ignored, and debate over public employment measures requires the clarification of the concept. "Public employment" is still used as a catch-all; to some people it is synonymous with entry-level jobs paying near poverty wages, offering few remedial services, and serving the hardcore unemployed. Others think of "public employment" in connection with better paying paraprofessional positions with upgrading potential for educated, lower-middle class minority group members. When federal funding is involved, the level and duration of support become crucial.

The usefulness of a public employment program cannot be meaningfully considered until the target population is identified, the type and intensity of remedial services are specified, the means of administration are determined, and the goals clearly articulated. Lessons from the past are vital in making all these distinctions. There have been public employment programs for disadvantaged youths, for family heads on welfare, for workers temporarily unemployed, and for older persons. Each of these has had necessarily different goals and content. Which of these has been most effective? Which are most needed in present circumstances? What is the impact of rapid implementation and how fast can slots be feasibly created? Does a wage subsidy encourage inefficiency by creating a supply of free labor, and in what form should the subsidies be provided? These and other questions can be at least partially answered by more careful evaluation of previous public employment programs. It is essential that such knowledge be used in making decisions about public employment programs for current conditions.

82

8

Expanding and Regulating Manpower Programs

THE RHETORIC: Manpower programs should continue to expand at a rapid pace, assuming a primary role in federal economic policy.

THE REALITY: There are constraints to expansion, and the importance of manpower programs among federal efforts is usually exaggerated.

One of the most widely accepted assumptions about the manpower effort is that it will continue to expand at a rapid pace. Since total enrollment thus far has been limited, including only a small proportion of the potential clientele, the extension of manpower services to all those in need is supposedly justified and will be forthcoming. With this expansion, manpower policy will assume a wider significance alongside the government's monetary and fiscal tools. It is on this note, for instance, that the *1970 Manpower Report* begins:

This Nation has had a growing commitment to manpower objectives and programs . . . With the rapid expansion of these programs in recent years, there has been an increasing awareness of their significance in contributing to economic as well as social objectives. As manpower programs continue to expand, their economic impact will become more and more pronounced, and it becomes necessary to incorporate an understanding of this impact into thinking about economic policy.

Despite these solemn pronouncements, it is not at all clear that the manpower programs can or should be markedly expanded, or that they have a large role to play in federal economic policy.

No verdict can be rendered about the overall impact of the manpower programs, nor should such a verdict be expected considering the recent origin and initial difficulties of the programs. Work Experience and Training was discontinued (though revived under new management and new title), while the Job Corps and out-of-school NYC were reduced in size because of negative appraisals. Vocational Rehabilitation definitely helps those with physical handicaps, but has done little for those with socioeconomic ills—as program administrators continue to emphasize physical rehabilitation and to disassociate their efforts from other manpower programs. Vocational Education is improving, but its offerings are still out of date and its approach sometimes inflexible. The employment service has streamlined its operations in some areas, but in others it is still controlled by an encrusted bureaucracy unresponsive to community needs. The MDTA program was considered a success by most evaluators, improving the employability and earnings of participants, and the JOBS program has opened private sector opportunities to many disadvantaged persons. On balance, those served by manpower programs have probably been helped, but there is no way of knowing whether some alternative use of manpower funds might not have been more beneficial to participants.

Past experience would be of little concern if methods were being improved based on this experience, and if emphasis had been and was being shifted to the more successful approaches. This, however, is not the case. Some improvements have been made, but in many cases changes have originated for political rather than programmatic reasons. Often improvements in design and administration have been undone by altered priorities. Though the changes and the new priorities may turn out to be for the best, there is no guarantee that the changes will improve services to clients, and it is certainly not safe at this time to predict any significant improvement in the performance of the manpower programs. In the end, expansion of the manpower programs must be based on disparate evidence and a general belief that they are worthwhile. There is no unequivocal "proof" that they have been effective, though there are certainly more grounds for reaching this conclusion than with efforts in other areas. But this conclusion reflects value judgments.

THE CONSTRAINTS ON EXPANSION

Whether or not past and present experiences justify expansion, there are constraints which will be felt to an ever greater degree. These are often overlooked, but they are surely obstacles to any further large-scale increases in the manpower effort.

One constraint is the lack of trained manpower to administer projects, a problem which will become more intense as administration is decentralized even if the programs are not expanded. Too often it is assumed that demand will create supply. As proof, many point to the fact that while there were only a handful of manpower "experts" ten years ago there are now many thousand. No doubt there has been an increase in competent personnel, but the administrative difficulties of the programs suggest that many of the instant experts are lacking adequate preparation. If the programs are continuously expanded, it is doubtful that personnel can be supplied to take care of needs.

Boosting salaries is one obvious way to attract additional administrative and technical talent to manpower programs, but this is effectively foreclosed by most state and muncipal pay practices. The prevailing low salary scales in most states offer little promise of attracting those with the skills needed to administer the expanded manpower programs or to take over new responsibilities in the planning and administration of programs. This problem is recog-

85

nized and improvements are being made, but there is a long way to go before most state and local salaries are competitive.

Another constraint may be the limited potential of voluntarism by individuals and especially by corporations recognizing their "social responsibility." In the 1960s, voluntary work by businessmen and civic leaders, contributions of time and money by corporations, and a variety of services provided by nonprofit groups added substantially to the impact of the manpower programs while adding little to their cost. But there is increasing evidence that the limits of such voluntary aid may already have been reached, and certainly that they cannot be expanded greatly. For instance, the JOBS program is very clearly shifting over to subsidized rather than voluntary hires, and recent surveys of businessmen have indicated that they are generally disappointed with the returns from their displays of "corporate citizenship."

The programs are also likely to be less effective as they are expanded to serve the more seriously disadvantaged. It is almost universally true that project administrators have "creamed" from among their intended clienteles, even if this meant serving the "best" of a prescribed group with serious problems. Certainly there are many persons who could be helped and could benefit more than those being served; but it is a safe assumption that a large-scale expansion would reduce the benefit/cost ratio of the programs as they serve a less select group, though such expansion may be a desirable goal on other grounds than cost-benefit measurements.

This is especially true when it is understood that much of the impact on earnings and employability has been the result of concentrating on a disadvantaged group and enhancing their ability to compete for existing jobs. There has undoubtedly been some displacement effect, where those trained under the manpower programs have taken the place of others who have not participated. If more of those in need were provided assistance, more would be competing for available jobs and a smaller proportion would benefit. Also, if increased assistance were given to disadvantaged and usually black workers, helping them to compete for the jobs held by whites, blue-collar antipathies would be further exacerbated, particularly in slack labor markets prevailing in many areas. Currently there are indications of growing discontent among this group, stemming not from slippage relative to white-collar workers, but rather from the loss of their position relative to blacks. Since these workers constitute such a large number, programs cannot be financed which will make much of a dent in their assumed problems. The "solution" of cutting back on efforts for the disadvantaged should be rejected, but political realities may make further rapid expansion untenable.

These constraints are not binding in any absolute way, but they suggest that the pace of expansion will have to be slower than that of the past decade. While manpower programs must still play a prominent role, there are reasons to suggest that this should not be an ever-expanding one.

First, it is reasonable to anticipate that the ravages of discrimination will be reduced. This is a basic goal of the manpower effort. Progress is also being made in the education of minority groups. To the extent that these succeed, there will be less need for remedial manpower services. If income subsidies are increased, and especially if they are extended to the working poor, the importance of manpower programs will necessarily diminish.

Second, the universe of need for manpower programs, or at least the universe of those who can effectively use their services, is not unlimited. Typically, it is subject to gross exaggeration. In making the case for expanded manpower efforts, the Labor Department estimates include the unemployed, underemployed, those not in the labor force but who would accept jobs, and the working poor or near poor.

This yields a staggering total of more than 7 million people who are supposedly candidates for manpower programs which presently serve less than half a million at any one time. And if the potential clientele of vocational rehabilitation is added, the "universe of need" rises to 11 million or more. Such estimates are unrealistic. The assertion that 11 million people need manpower services carries about the same weight as the claim that the half of all adults who did not complete high school need adult basic education. Everyone "needs" help in the sense that they would be better off if they had improved skills and were able to get better jobs. Realistically, however, the universe of need must be determined by considering the adequacy of alternative means of improvement, the availability of jobs to absorb all those who are trained, the number of people who are sufficiently dissatisfied with their current status to do something about it, and finally, the rate of incremental return in earnings resulting from the societal and individual investments. The realistic universe of need, calculated in light of these factors, can be only a small portion of all those counted by the official estimates.

Nevertheless, the number that could realistically benefit from manpower services is several times the number currently receiving assistance. The need for expanded efforts is relatively clearcut, especially in light of the current depressed state of the economy. The question is how rapidly the program can be expanded.

The rapid expansion in the last decade was a major cause of the shortcomings in the manpower effort. In particular, attempts to make rational decisions on the basis of carefully documented evidence were undermined, limiting the success of social experimentation. Even worse, the services themselves suffered, frequently impairing the efficient use of manpower resources. With all their imperfections the programs could be justified, since even poorly designed and administered services were better than none and the needs of those seeking help were pressing. Nonetheless, further expansion at accelerated rates is likely to raise countervailing forces which would subject manpower efforts to stringent criticism.

All this suggests that a realistic goal for the next decade should be one of measured expansion, perhaps at somewhere between the 5 and 10 percent annual increase of the past two years. The higher figure would more than double manpower expenditures by the end of the 1970s, to roughly $6.6 billion in fiscal 1980. There is no reason why expansion should necessarily be limited to 5 or 10 percent, but this gives an idea of the scale of probable activities.

MANPOWER PROGRAMS AND ECONOMIC POLICY

Manpower programs have been touted as a major ingredient of overall federal economic policies. The argument begins with the recognition that there is a necessary trade-off between price stability and unemployment. The experience of industrial nations has been that prices rise when aggregate demand is high, when employers are hiring to increase production, and when wages are rising as employers compete for scarce labor. Alternatively, prices fall or remain stable when demand is slack, and when unemployment is consequently rising. The trade-off between price changes and unemployment has shown a fair degree of statistical regularity over time, which has meant that monetary and fiscal policies influencing aggregate demand could only reduce unemployment by raising prices, or vice versa.

The theoretical attractiveness of manpower programs is that they can shift the terms of trade-off so that lower levels of unemployment can be achieved with less inflationary pressure. Rehabilitation and training programs, it is reasoned, reduce "structural unemployment" by preparing technologically displaced or educationally deficient workers for useful work. In addition to reducing unemployment, prices will be diminished to the degree that the social benefits of the training programs exceed their cost. Improved labor market services reduce the time lost between jobs and thus the level of unemployment. Greater mobility of workers helps fill job vacancies which would otherwise have contributed to rising prices in tight labor markets. Thus improved placement, counseling, outreach, and mobility-inducing measures reduce "frictional unemployment," resulting in a decline in both prices and unemployment. Finally, efforts to improve vocational training and counseling of workers and measures to boost the supply of skilled laborers remove labor bottlenecks and increase productivity by lowering unit labor costs.

These theoretical arguments are grounded in economic experience. Manpower programs do promise to improve the terms of trade-off between unemployment and inflation. But their impact

89

should be placed in the proper perspective; members of Congress, executive officials, and even economists have sometimes shared inflated notions about the potentialities of manpower programs. The fact is that the hoped-for improvements will be realized only over the long run; and even then, their impact may not be great. Currently, some 450,000 people are enrolled in Labor Department-funded manpower programs, compared with approximately 4.5 million unemployed and more than 85 million in the labor force. If past experience is any guide, a third of the enrollees will drop out of the programs, and more than half will show no benefits in employment and earnings. Improvements for those who are helped cover the initial costs only over the long run, and these improvements might be only slightly greater than would have been achieved by spending the manpower funds some other way.

Many other government expenditures, for instance agricultural price supports, have much more impact on the economy. The disproportionate attention given to manpower programs is, in no small measure, due to the ease with which their effects are integrated into the existing analytical framework. The manpower programs affect the supply and demand for labor which are the key factors underlying the trade-off between price changes and unemployment. The directions of their impact are clearcut on the basis of theoretical arguments, but this should not, as it often does, lead to misconceptions about the magnitude of the impact.

One manifestation of these misconceptions is the belief that manpower policy can be applied counter-cyclically to control economic fluctuations. Monetary and fiscal policies have been used with great success over the last two decades to eliminate the more pronounced fluctuations in economic activity which once seemed inevitable. But "minor" business cycles still exist. Real growth rates in the 1960s varied from 1.9 percent in 1960–61 and 2.4 percent in 1966–67, to 6.6 percent in 1961–62 and 6.4 percent in 1965–66. In early 1970, real GNP was actually declining, suggesting that postmortems for the business cycle may have been premature.

On the theory that every little bit helps, the limitations of manpower programs are no argument against their utilization as counter-cyclical measures to help temper these minor fluctuations.

As long as its proper role is understood, manpower policy could be used to "fine-tune" the economy, not only by varying the mix of manpower programs in response to economic fluctuations, but also by adjusting the level of expenditures. One way to do this is to provide for an automatic increase in manpower funds when unemployment passes a certain level. The Nixon administration proposed that allocations to manpower programs be boosted by 10 percent when unemployment reached 4.5 percent for three consecutive months. This trigger mechanism might be extended by additional boosts in manpower funds for increases in unemployment above 4.5 percent.

This would probably be a useful measure, for as unemployment increases, it is logical to expand the programs which aid its victims. While aggregate demand management can change the level of unemployment, the effects must filter down through the economy. Manpower expenditures, on the other hand, are directed specifically to those who are most in need of help. Dollar for dollar, manpower programs probably have more impact on unemployment than other types of spending, and expanding them may be the best way to help the unemployed. But there is a limit to the dollars which can be effectively spent under the manpower programs and to the resources which society will commit to this end.

It is doubtful whether manpower programs will ever become major counter-cyclical tools. For instance, if an unemployment rate increase of 1 percent triggered a 10 percent increase in manpower expenditures, roughly 45,000 additional slots could be created, given the current scale of programs—though it is doubtful that bonafide training slots could be created on short notice. This would fall far short of needs. A 1 percent rise in unemployment means that on the average 850,000 more workers will be out of jobs, and that the number of persons unemployed 15 weeks or longer during the course of the year will increase even more. Any reasonable expansion in manpower programs would absorb only a small proportion of a recession's victims; it is hardly a substitute for monetary and fiscal measures in controlling fluctuations. Manpower policy we must have, but we must not overestimate its efficacy in a slack economy.

9

The Implications of Social Experimentation

Social experimentation has been a relatively unique feature of the manpower effort, and its contributions have been significant. In the process, however, inflated claims have gone unchallenged and misconceptions allowed to continue, which exaggerate its impact. To appraise realistically the effects of measurement, evaluation, and experimental engineering, it is necessary to distinguish between the rhetoric and the reality of social experimentation. Such an approach is essentially negative, looking at the half-empty rather than half-filled cup; but it is unavoidable if the myths of manpower policy are to be dispelled so that the very real contributions that have been made to formulating and administering social policy will become clear.

FALSE CLAIMS AND MISCONCEPTIONS

The primary purpose of the manpower programs has been to solve problems and not to experiment with solutions. Only secondarily have they focused on testing alternative approaches and making policy formulation and implementation more rational. Because the real world is complex, and a number of factors influence the

92

success or failure of any effort, the lessons which have been learned are not unequivocal. No one can claim that any single approach has been a demonstrated success; only that it has done well in certain circumstances, at a given time, and administered in a particular way.

Despite the wealth of data which has been generated under the manpower programs, and the refined analytic techniques which have been applied, there are major shortcomings in measurement and evaluation. Data are unavailable to answer many important questions, especially to judge the long-run impact of manpower services and to identify their separate contributions. The analytical tools, such as cost-benefit analysis, cannot deliver straightforward measures of comparative effectiveness, and they are often misdirected in focusing attention on the wrong problems.

Despite these limitations, analysis of available data can help to identify problem areas and to suggest the needed directions of change. Yet there are obstacles to the implementation of these improvements, and the counsel of "experts" has often been ignored. In many cases, evaluation has been used as a pawn in political maneuvers, and vested groups have been able to delay actions which threaten their interests. Rarely has there been a direct cause and effect relationship between evaluation and action, since there is usually a wide gap between analysts and those with administrative and legislative responsibility. Mutual understanding will have to be improved so that the impact of measurement and evaluation will be enhanced.

The methods of experimentation have a part to play in determining priorities. By providing information about the needs of different groups and the effectiveness of alternative approaches, they give an idea of the trade-offs which must occur in the allocation of scarce resources. But this role is sometimes exaggerated. In changing or establishing priorities, it is a natural political reaction to suggest that the new thrusts are the product of careful experimentation, stemming from lessons learned in the past. This, at least, was the assertion underlying some recent changes in emphasis. Careful analysis of these issues suggests that the differing principles of the new administration had more to do with these priorities than the proved effectiveness of the emphasized approaches. It appears, in fact, that too little attention was given to evaluations of existing efforts.

Few manpower administrators and evaluators would question the need for administrative improvements. With the rapid proliferation and expansion of programs, there are duplications, gaps in coverage, and difficulties in coordinating separate approaches. Planning is especially difficult where so many people have their fingers in the pie. The problems are more severe at the state and local level complicated by shortages of skilled manpower and lack of control over the allocation of funds. And since there are no proven paths to improvement, concerned groups have been able to delay change and to defend their interests against any threatening changes, real or imaginary. By the time a compromise is reached, it is unlikely that the improvements will be more than marginal, at least in the short run. In this case evaluators have pinpointed the problems, but they have been unable to agree upon a solution or to get action.

Rising unemployment and declining economic opportunities are likely to alter dramatically the relative effectiveness of the manpower programs, and to place manpower policy in an entirely new perspective. On the assumption that the 1970 slump would be short-lived, most evaluators, administrators, and legislators saw no need for any major changes in strategy. Their implicit belief is that manpower programs will become more and not less important. Few have pressed for a careful examination of the programs' performance to determine the impact of the economic slump, or a re-examination of their past history to try to gather any insights this may offer. The rhetoric ignores the across-the-board effects which the high level of unemployment has had and will continue to have upon manpower programs.

One of the basic assumptions of social policy is that constructive efforts should be expanded to help all those in need. Almost everyone familiar with the manpower programs admits that the rapidity of their expansion in the 1960s was detrimental to their performance. But many assume that the ill effects of growth can be minimized as lessons are learned, and that expansion can continue, albeit at a more modest pace. The rhetoric of manpower policy stresses the meagerness of current efforts relative to the number of those who could benefit from manpower services. There is little discussion of the constraints on further expansion, and few attempts to determine the "optimum" rate of growth. When manpower policy is discussed along with monetary and fiscal policies, especially in the framework of the unemployment-inflation trade-off, this leaves an exaggerated impression of its impact. The error is one of omission rather than commission, in that the persons directing and evaluating the manpower programs have paid too little attention to the constraints and realities which limit their influence. In determining the resources committed to these goals, both sides of the picture must be weighed.

SUBSTANTIVE CONTRIBUTIONS

Though social experimentation has fallen short of the inflated expectations and claims which have been sustained by the rhetoric of manpower policy, it has generally had a favorable impact. Perhaps more than ever before, an attempt has been made to measure, evaluate, and feed back program results to test different approaches and hypotheses. Lessons have been learned even if they have not always been applied. Relative to progress elsewhere, these accomplishments stand out conspicuously. Though we know all too little about the long-run impact of manpower programs on their clientele, we know next to nothing about the benefits of increased education, a new defense system, or altered welfare procedures. Lacking concrete knowledge, efforts must be carried out on the basis of assumptions about their worth and their general design. Perhaps these can never be tested reliably. Whether increased college attendance today will prove to be a worthwhile investment will not be known for many years, if ever. Whether a new defense system serves a purpose may never be known; or worse, we may not be around to find out. In the manpower area, the programs have been better analyzed and evaluated, so that questions can at least be framed and partially answered.

Because so many factors have affected the formulation and administration of manpower policy, and because the lessons learned as a result of measurement and evaluation are diffuse, it is impossible to enumerate their contributions. In general, however, the social experimentation approach has yielded a fairly good picture of what the programs are doing, and some assessments of their success. Measurement and evaluation have helped to pinpoint problem areas and to suggest the most promising avenues for improvement. By providing facts rather than opinions, they have increased the rationality of decision-making, pushing back the boundaries of normative as opposed to objective choice.

Perhaps the most important contribution of social experimentation is the light it has shed on the underlying assumptions of manpower policy. This, in the end, is the major purpose of any experiment—to test the postulates on which it is based. As might be expected, no precise determinations have been made, since ideas are rarely "right" or "wrong." However, much has been learned about their ramifications and general validity.

In simplest form, the postulates of the manpower effort are: that people who can work should work; that jobs are available if workers are adequately prepared; that training and education can provide the needed preparation, even for those with severe problems; and that employment, increased income, and greater self-sufficiency will be worth far more in the long run than the cost of remedial attention.

Who Can Work?

Few would argue with the claim that those who can should work, but experience with the manpower programs has shown how difficult it is to define and identify employability and employable persons—or for that matter, what constitutes productive employment. For instance, should women on welfare work? This

96

depends on the number of children, their age, the availability of child-care facilities, and earnings potential. The "dude" on the street corner is a less questionable case from society's point of view, but experience with the manpower programs has made it quite clear that he will not take a dead-end job or participate in an unpromising program when hustling beckons. Should elderly persons be put to work when low-skill jobs must be created and when the payoff period on training is so short? For these and many more questions there are no simple answers, for we have learned that the Protestant ethic is difficult to apply in a society which offers alternative means of support.

The problem becomes especially acute in regard to current proposals to extend welfare payments to the working poor, while at the same time providing incentives so that these persons continue their employment. Incentives necessarily raise the cost of welfare and the range of incomes which are served, while they put downward pressure on the minimum payment made to the family whose head cannot work. When minimum support is offered to all, the corollary of the principle that those who can work should work is that those who do work should receive a decent wage. The boundaries between "workfare" and welfare are becoming increasingly vague if not completely obliterated, and this indicates the need to establish new rules about the universe of need applicable to manpower efforts.

JOBS FOR EVERYONE

The availability of jobs for those who are trained clearly depends on the health of the economy. The period between 1965 and 1969 was an ideal environment for an expanding manpower effort because the general level of unemployment was only a minor social problem. Public employment as a job creation strategy proved unnecessary except for the most disadvantaged among the hardest to employ groups, and a large majority of graduates from the manpower programs could find private sector employment. At the same time, this was a period of intense effort to break down racial discrimination, with profound implications for the disadvantaged participants in manpower programs.

The decline in economic conditions at the end of 1969 through 1970 demonstrated that such a favorable environment could not be assumed, and that in recession successful participation in manpower programs was not the "open sesame" it once might have been. The last hired in good times were the first to be fired as unemployment rose, while placements became more and more difficult. Large-scale public employment programs became more attractive when there were clear indications that private jobs were declining.

Even when jobs were plentiful, however, it was learned that job development and placement activities had to be closely linked with training if they were to succeed. There has been a noticeable shift in emphasis from programs which provide training as a preparation for later employment to those which "hire first and train later."

THE EMPLOYABILITY FORMULA

There is no single formula to determine in advance the services needed to make a person employable, and there is no guarantee that a selected combination will work. Experience with the manpower programs has shown that clients may need anything from a label as "disadvantaged" which will make them attractive to socially conscious firms, to extensive basic education before any job training can even begin. There are many jobs which require little or no special training, while for others the needed skills are so specific that they must be provided at high cost on the job. The problem is to determine what mix of services a particular client may need, and much remains to be learned in this area. It is still not known with any certainty when training or education outside of a particular job will increase employability, or when on-the-job training will have benefits which carry over to other work situations.

An even more basic question is the extent of remedial training and education efforts needed to prepare severely disadvantaged workers at acceptable per capita costs for more than just entry jobs. Most programs have concentrated on preparing these persons for entry-level positions and have generally chosen those for whom employability is within easy reach. Many of the jobs for which manpower services were provided could have been filled without preparation; questions have justifiably been raised about the quality of training offered for sanitation work, janitorial services, "aide" positions, and other unskilled jobs. On the other hand, after a brief experiment with intensive vocational training for the severely disadvantaged in the Job Corps, it was decided that this concentration of resources was not warranted; the program was judged too costly because of the extensive groundwork which had to be laid. Training opportunities in the Job Corps were sharply curtailed, though the rhetoric about upgrading the disadvantaged was intensified.

While shortcomings in the programs or the availability of more attractive alternatives are partially responsible for the high drop-out rates experienced by the manpower programs, these rates also attest to the difficulty if not impossibility of preparing many for work. Established education and training institutions must be assigned the blame for failing to provide for the needs of large groups in the population, but many individuals have failed in the past because they lack ability. To assume that all can be rehabilitated is naive. The Job Corps experience has offered ample evidence that individuals who experienced educational problems during their first round in school—whether because the school system failed them or because they just failed—tend to have serious difficulties when they are offered a second chance to acquire an education. Male Job Corps enrollees averaged a fifth grade level of achievement, and the time and cost needed to bring them up to a "functional" level would be considerable. A year of intensive education raised achievement level of enrollees by less than the school norm. Opportunities to participate in vocational and basic education programs, combined with other manpower services, can increase the employability of many; but the mix of offerings must be carefully tailored to the individual, and even then success is not assured.

THE PAYOFF ON MANPOWER PROGRAMS

The manpower efforts were expanded in the belief that benefits would exceed costs. Today, despite a number of careful studies of individual programs and their performance, this remains an article of faith rather than a proved fact. While participants have increased their employability and earnings on the average and the programs have definitely had a favorable effect as a whole, there is no way of predicting their long-run impact or of weighting discounted benefits against aggregate costs. The $12 billion spent on manpower efforts during the 1960s is not inconsequential, attesting to the high costs of remedial efforts.

Some would suggest the expansion of manpower services to all those in need. Others feel that emphasis should be given to preventive rather than remedial measures. The argument is appealing, but evidence is lacking that increased expenditures on education and training the first time around will preclude the needs of future remedial efforts.

Other alternatives to manpower programs are available. Income subsidies can be expanded in lieu of increasing earnings, or monetary and fiscal policies might be used to drive unemployment rates to lower levels at the cost of intensified inflationary pressures. The choice of the strategies can be improved by the insights gained from the manpower programs, but it remains in the final analysis a matter of political preference and personal values.

A LITTLE KNOWLEDGE

The old adage asserts that a little knowledge can be a dangerous thing, and this applies to manpower programs. Measurement and evaluation can lead to disillusionment about the effectiveness of the manpower programs as a whole, causing the shifting of resources to other areas where promises are not denied by the facts. If the harsh light of analysis which illuminates manpower policies were focused elsewhere, the effects could be withering. On the other hand, the little knowledge which is available can be misused for advocacy purposes. Measurement and evaluation might be perverted to support the indiscriminate expansion of manpower programs and specific measures may be altered or expanded unjustifiably on the basis of manufactured evidence offered under the guise that the recommendations are the product of careful experimentation.

Limited knowledge does not have to have negative consequences: the insights gained by careful measurement, evaluation, and feedback can be important supplements to rule-of-thumb judgments, political decision-making, and compromises among vested interests. No claim is made that analytical tools played a crucial role in past design and implementation of programs, or that they will make a much greater contribution in the future. However, the influence of rhetoric surrounding manpower policy can be minimized if the potentials of measurement and evaluation are better understood. This requires that present limitations of our knowledge about manpower programs be explicitly stated.

Evaluators and program analysts must make it crystal clear to policy shapers that we know very little about the impact of most programs and that the crude state of our knowledge is likely to prevail for some time, indeed for the foreseeable future. Data are scarce, especially concerning the exact services which are offered and their long-run impact. It is difficult and costly to track any single individual through the maze of manpower services. The means of separating the effect of various services are crude or nonexistent. The assessments applicable under one set of conditions may not hold true in a different place or time. There are few, if any, eternal verities involved in manpower policy.

Despite these limitations, existing data might have been used more effectively if research funds were not under the control of program administrators. Instead, manpower funds allocated to research and evaluation are another "rice bowl" coveted by resident scholars, academicians, and the sprouting, lucrative manpower research enterprises. Evaluations have been for the most part either in-house and inclined to advocacy rather than objectivity—or under contract with administrative agencies, in which case vacuity (adorned by academic jargon and embellished by a dose of "scientific" mathematical formulation) passes for rigid analysis and has its own rewards.

Compared with our knowledge about the programs, our understanding of their underlying approaches is diminutive. While there might be some agreement about the relative success and failure of programs, even the best informed observers are rarely able to distinguish the components accounting for the results. Available evaluations have focused on the total impact of programs and have tended to ignore the effect of different services and approaches on diverse groups. A change of perspective is needed. Programs must be judged explicitly on the basis of the clientele they are serving, and relative to alternative methods of helping these same persons. The underlying assumptions must be tested and not merely the program forms.

All this should by now be obvious. What remains to be seen is whether improvements can in fact be made to increase the effectiveness of social experimentation, and if this can be done, whether it is worth the trouble.

IMPROVING EXPERIMENTAL METHODS

It is much easier to describe problems than to prescribe viable solutions, but the admitted difficulties to understanding the underlying processes should not discourage added efforts. Though the task is not an easy one, the previous analysis suggests some directions in which we should move:

1. An increasing proportion of funds for research and evaluation must be provided independently of administrative and advocate agencies. Congress need not depend exclusively upon executive agencies for information about program operations. It could demand and obtain needed data by sustained funding or through the General Accounting Office and its own Legislative Reference

Service. This is extremely important if the knowledge which is gained through experimentation is to be applied. Congress should also demand that review of program developments in the annual *Manpower Report* be strengthened to become more than an apologia for administration policies. Public review by Congressional committees can be helpful, but in the final analysis Congress must develop its own independent source for checking and evaluating the efforts for which it expends public funds.

2. Funds must also be made available for studies broaching more than one program, focusing on their common experiences rather than their programmatic differences. For instance, studies should be made of the need for and usefulness of counseling, health care, basic and vocational education, placement, and other services for different groups. Projects should be set up to test the value of all the component services offered under a program, and research must focus on why a program works in one area and not another.

3. More reliable data need to be gathered about program achievements by carefully tracing the pre- to post-enrollment experience of each participant. Follow-up investigations should be institutionalized while control groups should be selected and observed throughout the operation of every program as part of its research function.

4. Cost-benefit techniques must be increasingly supplemented by other tools of analysis. The interdisciplinary approach should be used more widely, and numerologists should not be allowed to supplant common-sense evaluators who synthesize a variety of tools, including public opinion samplings, journalistic sources, gumshoe investigations, budget and Congressional information, sociological and psychological findings, as well as cost-benefit studies.

5. Before program evaluations will become meaningful or comparable, obvious shortcomings in planning, coordination, and administration must be overcome. Care must be taken, however, that oversight and control do not become lost as a result of the consolidation of separate program authorities, and that the requirements for planning and evaluation are strictly enforced, which has rarely been the case under other block grant programs.

103

6. More attention must be given to improving the quality of manpower evaluators and administrators. With the rapid growth in the past, almost anyone could qualify as an "expert" by gaining administrative authority or by staking an early academic claim. The Labor Department funds manpower institutes in each of its ten regions and is supporting doctoral candidates who are preparing dissertations on manpower subjects; these promising efforts should be expanded.

7. Changes in emphasis and approach must become less drastic, and a longer-run perspective must be taken in judging program performance. Less emphasis should be given to instant success; more patience should be cultivated to permit long-range evaluation of programs. Funds should also be provided to investigate programs which have been tried and abandoned to clarify their lessons and to avoid repetition of mistakes.

8. If unemployment levels off at higher rates, as it might, existing programs and approaches must be carefully reexamined to determine their effectiveness under these conditions. Flexibility must be encouraged in adapting to changed circumstances, but care must be taken not to overreact. Most of all, the spirit of social experimentation must be reinvoked as the manpower programs begin to operate in a new environment.

9. In the 1970s, manpower programs will hopefully be developed without the crash implementation which wasted resources and postponed measurement and evaluation during the 1960s. The constraints to expansion must be given adequate consideration, and manpower policy should not be forced to assume a role in federal economic policy for which it is ill-equipped. Anticipations that manpower programs can be manipulated to assume a countercyclical role, for example, should not receive great emphasis until more evidence is generated that this is a viable function.

THE BIGGEST RICE BOWL OF ALL

The effectiveness of any social program will be improved to the extent that its goals are made explicit, its performance measured and evaluated relative to these goals, and its design and implementation altered in light of these evaluations. "Social experimentation" means that programs will be administered with these aims in mind.

Despite the many shortcomings which have been noted, the greater emphasis on social experimentation under the manpower programs than under other federally-funded measures has contributed to improved performance. Measured against inflated claims, the impact of social experimentation has been meager. Measured relative to its impact elsewhere, it has been substantial.

Nonetheless, measurements, evaluation, and experimentation have not been costless, and it is pertinent to ask whether the payoff has made them worthwhile. Though changes which have been suggested may potentially improve the impact of manpower programs, there is no assurance that the suggested reforms will be implemented or that they would result in the hoped-for improvements. The worth of experimental methods must be judged on their impact in the past, and this has been disappointing to many.

Critics of "academic frills" have charged that little has been accomplished and that additional studies will not improve program performance or help overcome demonstrated obstacles. As a public official once stated, he was not inclined to spend good public money to find out why fried potatoes became brown. Even with the best of data, the techniques of evaluation can yield only vague answers to hard questions, since it is difficult to discern causes and effects in social matters. Because the political facts of life and accommodations among other interest groups must always be faced, objective measurement and evaluation, no matter how good it is, will have to compete with other vital considerations in decision-making processes.

On the other hand, advocates might rightfully claim that while prescriptions are never exact or absolute, analysis can indicate what a program is doing and what must be done to improve its performance, given a set of explicit objectives. Though the lessons which are learned may not be implemented, they cannot be ignored; eventually, proved facts will carry the day and policies will be shaped by their analyses rather than by anecdotes.

105

The truth is that neither of these arguments can be refuted. There is no way of knowing what the manpower programs would have accomplished if less emphasis had been placed on social experimentation, and less money spent on measurement, evaluation, and demonstration projects. The impact of research and analysis cannot be judged by the aggregation of incidents where analytic advice was or was not heeded. Rather than playing a leading role, objective analysis helped set the stage on which social, political and economic factors operated. It is equally difficult to estimate the costs of this effort. Research and evaluation are privately as well as publicly funded, and when absorbed into the administration of programs, their price tag is often obscured. Demonstrations and experiments accomplish purposes outside of the knowledge they generate, and to charge their whole cost to research is misleading. Thus, there is no way to accurately estimate the costs or benefits of social experimentation. The frequently repeated assertion that social experimentation has been worthwhile remains an assumption—one which is obviously self-serving. The admission casts suspicion on the conclusion that measurement, evaluation, and experimentation of manpower efforts should be intensified. Whatever our motivation, we remain convinced that the clients of manpower programs will be helped if policy shapers are persuaded to make the conclusion a reality.

Appendix

FEDERALLY ASSISTED

Program Title and Authorizing Legislation	Target Population	Services Provided	Persons Served (thousands)		
			1968 actual	1969 actual	1970 estimate
MDTA Institutional Training Manpower Development and Training Act of 1962, Title II	Mostly unemployed, 16 years of age and over, underutilized workers for upgrading, 2/3 disadvantaged	Occupational training or retraining in a classroom setting at a school or Skill Center; includes testing, counseling, selection, job development, referral and job placement.	140	135	148
MDTA On-the-Job Training (OJT)[1] Manpower Development and Training Act of 1962, Title II	Mostly unemployed, preference for 18 year olds and over, 1/2 disadvantaged	Instruction and supervised work at the job site; may include classroom training at vocational education institution or employer's location.	125	130	130
Job Corps Economic Opportunity Act of 1964, Title I-A	School dropouts, 16 to 21 years of age, family below poverty level, youth from area with no training opportunities readily accessible	Residential setting with intensive education, skill training, counseling, and related services.	65	53	47
Neighborhood Youth Corps (NYC) In-School and Summer	In-school youth, 16 to 21 years of age, family below poverty level	Part time employment and work experience, some counseling.	324	429	445
Out-of-School Economic Opportunity Act of 1964, Title I-B	Out-of-school youth, 16 to 18 years of age, family below poverty level	Skill training, remedial education, work experience, counseling, health care.	94	74	37
New Careers[2] Economic Opportunity Act of 1964, Title I-B	Disadvantaged adults and out-of-school youths	Work experience and training in human service field; includes basic education, counseling and related services.	12	15	20
Operation Mainstream Economic Opportunity Act of 1964, Title I-B	Chronically unemployed poor, 22 years of age and over, mainly from rural areas	Job creation and work training in community improvement and beautification projects; includes counseling, basic education, etc.	13	11	11
Public Service Careers (PSC) Manpower Development and Training Act of 1962 Economic Opportunity Act of 1964, Title I-B	Disadvantaged adults and youth, underutilized workers for upgrading	Subsidies to State and local public service agencies for employment, training, and upgrading costs	—	4	18
Special Impact Economic Opportunity Act of 1964, Title I-D	Unemployed in poor urban and rural areas	Manpower training as a component of economic and community development programs	*Not available*		
Job Opportunities in the Business Sector (JOBS) Manpower Development and Training Act of 1962 Economic Opportunity Act of 1964	Hard-core unemployed and under-employed, 18 years of age and over, working disadvantaged for upgrading	Orientation, counseling, job related education, minor medical and day care, on-the-job training	107	136	156

MANPOWER PROGRAMS

Expenditures (millions)			Eligible Contractors or Sponsors	Agencies and Their Roles	Trainee Allowances
1968 actual	1969 actual	1970 estimate			
$203	$197	$205	Skill Centers, public or private schools	U.S. Training and Employment Service determines needs and renders supportive services. Dept. of Health, Education, and Welfare administers training through State educational system. Dept. of Labor, Unemployment Insurance Service provides training allowances and subsistence payments.	Adult—$10 above average weekly Unemployment Benefits in state, $5 for each of 4 dependents. Youth—$20 per week.
67	70	70	National unions, multi-plant companies, trade associations, public agencies	U.S. Training and Employment Service administers through agreements with employers and other organizations.	Receives wage from employer
318	258	180	Conservation Centers—federal and state agencies, Regional and Residential Centers—non-profit organizations, public agencies, private businesses	Dept. of Labor assumed responsibility from the Office of Economic Opportunity in fiscal 1970. Governor must approve location of any Center in his state.	$30 to $50 per month plus $5 adjustment allowance
198	182	212	State and local government agencies, community action agencies, public institutions such as hospitals and schools	U.S. Training and Employment Service administers through contracts with Prime Sponsors in Community Program areas, and other sponsors.	$1.45 per hour In school maximum 15 hours Summer—25 to 30 hours
143	106	100	Same as In-School, but may include profit-making organizations	U.S. Training and Employment Service administers through contracts with local sponsors.	3/4 of local MDTA allowance All of MDTA allowance for head of household
24	35	38	Private non-profit and public agencies	Program now incorporated into Public Service Careers Program administered by U.S. Training and Employment Service.	Employment at minimum wage
31	37	41	Community action agencies in specially designated areas	U.S. Training and Employment Service administers through Prime Sponsors in Community Program areas.	Minimum federal or local wage
—	17	60	Federal, State and local government agencies, private non-profit and public agencies	U.S. Training and Employment Service administers through Prime Sponsors in Community Program areas or through contracts with other sponsors. This program incorporates the New Careers Program.	Employment at minimum wage for new hires and higher for upgraded workers
6	22	31	Community action agencies, public and non-profit agencies	Office of Economic Opportunity administers through grants to community development corporations.	*Not available*
68	104	192	Private profit or non-profit organizations, boards of trade, chambers of commerce	U.S. Training and Employment Service provides supportive services. National Alliance of Businessmen, through 131 offices, promotes cooperation of industry nationwide.	Receives wage from employer

FEDERALLY ASSISTED

Program Title and Authorizing Legislation	Target Population	Services Provided	Persons Served (thousands) 1968 actual	1969 actual	1970 estimate
Concentrated Employment Program (CEP) Manpower Development and Training Act of 1962 Economic Opportunity Act of 1964	Disadvantaged persons in 82 urban poverty and rural deprived areas, predominately male enrollees	Coordinated delivery of manpower, supportive services	68	140	189
Work Incentive Program (WIN) Social Security Amendments of 1967	Recipients of aid to families with dependent children	Training work experience, job creation, basic education, orientation, child care, transportation	—	33	138
Federal State Employment Service[3] Wagner-Peyser Act of 1933 Social Security Act of 1935	Entire labor force, predominately the unemployed, disadvantaged	Recruitment, testing, placement and job market information	5,760	5,524	4,600
Vocational Education[4] Vocational Education Act of 1963, as amended	School age youth for technical occupations, 2/5 for adults and youths from low income families, the physically or mentally handicapped.	Training for employment as semi-skilled or skilled worker, and for business or office occupations	5,534	6,034	6,543
Vocational Rehabilitation Vocational Rehabilitation Act of 1920	Physically, mentally, or socially handicapped	Counseling, guidance, therapy, training, placement, and follow-up	330	368	432
Apprenticeship[5] National Apprenticeship Act of 1935	Persons under 26 years of age ordinarily, for occupations considered apprenticeable	Technical assistance to employers, labor unions, and community organizations in developing and administering apprenticeship programs, and increasing opportunities for minorities	78	110	105
Adult Basic Education (ABE) Adult Basic Education Act of 1966, Title III	Adults 16 years of age and over who have not attained an 8th grade level of education	Elementary instruction in reading, writing, and computation skills	408	532	590
Project 100,000 Military Service Acts	Potential inductees with low academic achievement or remediable physical defects	Qualifies men for military service who would not ordinarily be accepted	—	87	62
Transition National Defense Act of 1916	Military personnel with approximately 6 months of active duty remaining; emphasis on those with job handicaps	Counseling, basic education, skill training, and job placement in civilian employment	80	170	300

MANPOWER PROGRAMS (cont'd)

Expenditures (millions) 1968 actual	1969 actual	1970 estimate	Eligible Contractors or Sponsors	Agencies and Their Roles	Trainee Allowances
54	127	152	Community action agencies, state employment services	U.S. Training and Employment Service administers through contracts with Prime Sponsors in Community Program areas or other local sponsors while providing supportive services.	Varies with program enrollee enters
—	81	133	State employment services	Dept. of Health, Education, and Welfare, through welfare agencies, refers clients to state employment services which sponsor local projects.	Varies with program enrollee enters
312	317	350	State employment services	U.S. Training and Employment Service through affiliated state employment service agencies.	None
258	259	285	State education agencies, colleges, university, and other institutions (research)	Dept. of Health, Education, and Welfare, Office of Education, administers through grants to States and territories. Research administered by Commissioner of Education through contracts and grants to states and institutions.	None
281	351	478	State rehabilitation agencies, colleges, universities, and other institutions (research)	Dept. of Health, Education and Welfare, Social and Rehabilitation Service, administers through State vocational rehabilitation agencies.	Provides $25 per week for an individual with $10 per dependent to a maximum of four; limited to special workshop projects
6	9	7	State apprenticeship agencies U.S. Bureau of Apprenticeship and Training	Bureau of Apprenticeship and Training administers through state apprenticeship agencies and/or its own staff in each state.	Receives wage from employer
39	45	55	State and local education agencies, public or private non-profit organizations (research)	Dept. of Health, Education and Welfare, Office of Education, administers through grants to State and local public school systems. Commissioner of Education administers research, demonstration, and ABE staff training grants.	None
—	10	7	Department of Defense	Dept. of Defense administers at induction centers and military installations.	Receives regular military pay
8	14	15	Department of Defense	Department of Defense administers at military installations in cooperation with the Dept. of Labor, HEW/OE, and other Federal agencies.	Receives regular military pay

1 In fiscal 1971 OJT will be combined with Job Opportunities in the Business Sector (JOBS).
2 New Careers has been incorporated into the Public Service Careers program for fiscal 1971.
3 Data entered under persons served represent total number of non-farm placements by local employment service agenci
4 Figures entered for persons served represent total enrollment, i.e., students supported by federal and non-federal resource Expenditures, however, relate to federal assistance only.
5 The number of new entrants into registered apprenticeship programs during each year appears in the chart as persons serve
Sources: Office of Management and Budget, U.S. Department of Labor, Supp. No. 29, Bureau of National Affairs, Ma power Information Service, Oct. 21, 1970, pp. 21:1006–9.